THE WELFARE OF EUROPE'S CHILDREN

Are EU member states converging?

John Micklewright and Kitty Stewart

The POLICY PRESS

United Nations Children's Fund
Innocenti Research Centre
Florence - Italy

First published in Great Britain in April 2000 by

The Policy Press
University of Bristol
34 Tyndall's Park Road
Bristol BS8 1PY
UK

Tel +44 (0)117 954 6800
Fax +44 (0)117 973 7308
E-mail tpp@bristol.ac.uk
http://www.bristol.ac.uk/Publications/TPP

© UNICEF, 2000

ISBN 1 86134 226 8

John Micklewright is Head of Research at UNICEF Innocenti Research
Centre, Florence, Italy. He was previously Professor of Economics at Queen
Mary and Westfield College, London, and at the European University Institute.
Kitty Stewart is Research Officer at UNICEF Innocenti Research Centre,
Florence, Italy. She took her Doctorate in Economics from the European
University Institute.

Front cover: Photograph supplied by kind permission of The Children's Society
Cover design by Qube Design Associates, Bristol
Printed in Great Britain by Hobbs the Printers Ltd, Southampton

Contents

List of tables and figures

Tables

Figures

Acknowledgements

This book is one of the outputs of a UNICEF Innocenti Research Centre project on 'EMU and Children'. (See also the paper by Atkinson, 1998a.) The project was financed by the core funding of the Italian Government to the Centre and through additional funding from the UNICEF Office for Europe (we thank Bilge Ogun-Bassani for her support and encouragement). We thank Tony Atkinson, Jonathan Bradshaw, Nuala O'Donnell, Hannele Sauli and participants in seminars at the London School of Economics, York, Hamilton and Kiawah for comments on draft material; Bruce Bradbury, Tony Atkinson and James Foster for discussion of issues in Chapter 2; Vijay Verma for information on mean incomes from the European Community Household Panel (ECHP) and Bruce Bradbury and Markus Jäntti for estimates of child poverty rates used in Chapter 3; Markus Jäntti and Nicola Madge for references for the discussion of youth suicide in Chapter 4; Robert Zimmermann for copy-editing suggestions and for checking the references; Eve leckey for her help with the proofs and other aspects of the publication process. We are very grateful to Nuala O'Donnell for research assistance with the Eurobarometer data used in Chapter 7. Cinzia Iusco Bruschi gave excellent administrative and secretarial support, as always. Lastly, we thank Dawn Rushen and her colleagues at The Policy Press for their smooth handling of the final production.

ONE

Introduction

The introduction of a single currency in most of the European Union (EU) in January 1999 saw great attention paid to the process of convergence among member states in a handful of macroeconomic indicators: inflation, the government deficit, the national debt, and long-term interest rates. Interest in these indicators has been natural since their convergence was required for participation in monetary union under the terms of the 1992 Maastricht Treaty; a requirement, in turn based on the idea that the single currency would not survive if it were introduced across economies which did not resemble each other in fundamental ways.

However, national performance in the EU risks being judged excessively on such macroeconomic criteria. Monetary union, a conclusion of the convergence process, is just a tool to reach a further end of increasing human welfare in Europe – as the Treaty on Union puts it, "the raising of the standard of living and quality of life" (Article 2). The Maastricht criteria should not divert attention from measuring progress towards these goals directly. And not only is the average level of well-being in Europe of concern, or that in particular countries, but also whether well-being is becoming more similar across member states as a whole – whether it is *converging*. Reduction of disparities in well-being among member states is at the heart of the European project. In this book we ask whether that is the direction in which we are moving, focusing on the situation of children. Is the welfare of children in the Union's member states becoming more or less similar over time?[1]

To some extent this sort of measurement of trends in human welfare in the EU does already take place. While it is macroeconomic convergence that has received the most attention, the Maastricht Treaty also called prominently for "the strengthening of economic and social cohesion", so as to promote the Union's "overall harmonious development" (Articles 2 and 130a). The Treaty established a Cohesion Fund to help those countries with relatively low GDP per capita: Greece, Ireland, Portugal and Spain – the so-called 'Cohesion Four'. And it gave the European Commission the task of preparing a report on economic and social cohesion every three years. The first of these reports was published in the mid-1990s (European Commission, 1996). But it concentrated on a fairly narrow concept of well-being: income and employment[2]. Other analyses of cohesion in the Union, for example Sala-i-Martin (1996a, 1996b) and Quah (1997a, 1997b) have had a similar focus. In this book we take a wider view of development and of individual well-being, more similar, for example, to that taken by the United Nations Development Programme's (UNDP's) *Human Development Reports*.

Why children? The nearly 80 million children in the Union aged under 18 represent over a fifth of the total EU population (see Table 1.1). Many other people of course live with children and are directly concerned with their well-being. Figure 1.1 shows the proportion of households for 12 EU countries that have a child aged 0-18 (the data do not identify the 0-17 years age range of Table 1.1). The average figure is one third. In Spain and Ireland over 40% of households contain a child[3]. Besides their importance viewed in this way, it is very obviously the case that the nature of children's progress to becoming tomorrow's adults helps determine the shape of Europe's future. Convergence in well-being across the Union as part of its 'overall harmonious development' means moving towards similar opportunities for European children wherever they are born[4].

Figure 1.1: EU households with children aged 0-18 (%)

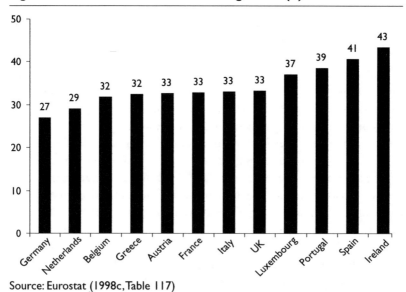

Source: Eurostat (1998c, Table 117)

Table 1.1: Children in Europe (1996)

	Children aged 0-17	
	Number **(000s)**	**Share of population** **(%)**
Austria	1,686	20.9
Belgium	2,190	21.6
Denmark	1,105	21.0
Finland	1,166	22.8
France	13,650	23.4
Germany	15,903	19.4
Greece	2,191	20.9
Ireland	1,084	30.0
Italy	10,521	18.4
Luxembourg	90	21.8
Netherlands	3,402	22.0
Portugal	2,191	22.1
Spain	8,218	20.9
Sweden	1,967	22.3
UK	13,529	23.1
EU 15	78,892	21.2

Source: Eurostat (1997f)

In Chapter 2 we define our concept of child welfare, relating this to the wider notion of human development. We define a vector of indicators but in contrast to the construction of the UNDP's Human Development Index we make no attempt to aggregate these into a summary measure. We also define our meaning of 'convergence'. Chapters 3 to 7 then deal in turn with our various dimensions of child welfare, investigating whether different parts of the EU have become more or less similar over time. We look at the economic well-being of children, at mortality, education, teenage fertility, and at young people's own views of their lives. The period we consider typically covers the last 15–25 years. (For practical reasons our analysis is at the level of the member state rather than at the finer level of the region that has been the focus of much of the literature on convergence of incomes[5].)

Chapter 8 concludes with the following questions: Are the dimensions of child welfare examined in the book converging over time? Do they at least show improvement, even on average? – is the welfare of Europe's children rising? This final chapter summarises what we have discovered.

It also points to the further data and analysis that are needed to put children at the heart of discussion on Europe's future.

Notes

[1] Our focus is on outcomes and not on policies. There is a large separate strand of inquiry that considers trends in the latter, including policies with a direct bearing on children. See, for example, Ruxton (1996), Sykes and Alcock (1998), and the work of the European Observatory on National Family Policies (Ditch et al, 1998).

[2] The report itself refers to its investigation of trends in incomes and employment as being a "traditional analysis of the relative circumstances of Europe's population" (European Commission, 1996, p 46), although some discussion is devoted to other dimensions of cohesion and it is clearly noted that income and employment are "insufficient in themselves to assess the full situation" (p 46).

[3] We were not able to find information on a comparable basis for EU countries that shows the proportion of *persons* living in households in which there are children, which will be substantially higher than the proportion of all households with children given in Figure 1.1. Jenkins (1999, Table 4) reports a figure of 51% for Britain (defining a child as less than 17 years old).

[4] There is no direct mention of children in the Maastricht Treaty and only one in the 1997 Amsterdam Treaty (in the context of cooperation to safeguard children from crime), although children do figure implicitly in references to policies on such matters as education. Similarly, although children are not singled out in the *First report on economic and social cohesion*, young people (together with women and the long-term unemployed) are noted as a particular target for cohesion policies in the employment field (European Commission, 1996, p 116). The report also expresses concern for "inter-generational cohesion" (p 46) in relation to the environmental consequences of economic growth.

[5] For example, the *First report on economic and social cohesion* presents analyses at both country and regional level (European Commission, 1996).

TWO

Concepts of child well-being and of convergence

How may child welfare be measured in the countries of the EU, given that we wish to track its changes over time? We begin by discussing appropriate indicators, before turning to consider how differences between countries and convergence over time may be judged with the indicators selected.

Child well-being in industrialised countries

The view that human welfare cannot be adequately measured by traditional indicators of economic development such as GDP per capita became widely voiced in the 1970s and subsequently developed into first the 'basic needs' and then the 'capabilities' approaches (for example Streeten and Burki, 1978; Sen, 1985, 1992). Both reject GDP as the sole indicator of well-being not just as an aggregate measure that is blind to the distribution of income, but also on the grounds that income itself is only one of the assets a person needs in order to lead what Sen has called "a good life". In the capabilities approach a good life is defined in terms of human 'functioning': what is important is that an individual has the "capability to achieve functionings that he or she has reason to value" (Sen, 1992, p 5). These functionings might include "such elementary things as being adequately nourished, being in good health, avoiding escapable morbidity and premature mortality, etc." as well as "more complex achievements such as being happy, having self-respect, taking part in the life of the community, and so on" (Sen, 1992, p 39). The UNDP *Human Development Reports*, first published in 1990, represent the best known attempt to select specific indicators of these functionings with the aim of comparing human welfare across countries according to wider criteria than GDP. They illustrate that the correlation between national income and a broader concept of well-being is far from perfect.

However, for obvious reasons, the focus of most attempts to measure human well-being has been the developing world, and the indicators used naturally reflect this: UNDP's Human Development Index has helped make basic literacy and life expectancy widely accepted as key welfare indicators, for instance. Attempts to measure the well-being of children have tended to have the same focus: in UNICEF's *The state of the world's children* (1998) the basic indicators are infant and under-5 mortality and primary school enrolment, measures on which one would expect there to be little to separate European countries by the mid-1990s.

The fact that children in industrialised countries are now protected from many of the urgent problems affecting children in poorer parts of the world does not place these children beyond concern; rather, it means that additional measures of their welfare are needed. Other issues demand more attention once the basic problems of survival are overcome. And, at the same time, growing wealth brings with it new dangers as well as new opportunities.

A number of recent studies have identified this need to develop measures of well-being for children in richer countries. One ongoing project, sometimes referred to as the 'Jerusalem Initiative', has held three conferences aimed at coming up with a list of such indicators appropriate for cross-country comparison (see Ben-Arieh and Wintersberger, 1997, for the output of the first[1]). Hauser et al (1997) report on a similar initiative limited to the USA[2]. Both these studies face the same two problems: the need to choose a limited number of indicators of the almost endless array of values and failings we would like to measure once survival is more or less assured; and the need to reconcile the choice with the hard truth about what data do exist.

The second of these problems is a particular restriction where international comparison is concerned: studies of a single country do not have to worry about cross-country differences in measurement or availability of data (although availability and methods may certainly change over time). Nor is the analysis disturbed by differences in cultural approach to a range of issues from education to institutional care.

As yet, then, there is no consensus about the best set of indicators to use in an international comparison of child well-being in the industrialised world. Nor is a study of child well-being in Europe free of the constraints of data availability and differences in methods of measurement. Indeed, this turns out to be a perhaps surprisingly large obstacle. The EU has its own statistical agency, Eurostat, dedicated to providing comparative data for each of the member states. However, while Eurostat provides extensive comparative information on many aspects of life in Europe, relatively little attention is paid to childhood[3].

The statistical agencies of the member states of course produce a great deal of information on children through their various publications (for example CSO, 1994, in the case of the UK) but inevitably it is hard to gather consistent data from these on many topics.

Our task in this book is further complicated by our interest in *convergence*, which demands a time-series for each indicator. Eurostat's concentration on current members of the Union means that publications and databases prior to 1994 focus on the EU 12 rather than the 15 and so on (although some important retrospective analyses are made). The need for a time-series also rules out reliance on a number of other interesting potential sources which so far provide only a snapshot portrait of the situation in different countries or which provide series that cover too few countries. (Examples are the recent WHO Health of Youth Surveys [WHO, 1996b], the OECD International Adult Literacy Survey [OECD, 1995, 1997a], and the International Association for the Evaluation of Educational Achievement (IEA) assessments of maths and science [Beaton et al, 1996a, 1996b].)

The indicators of child well-being we look at in this book thus represent a compromise between what we would like to measure and what we can measure. Drawing on a variety of data sources – Eurostat, Eurobarometer, WHO, OECD and UNESCO – we have put together a range of indicators which cover various aspects of child well-being, but not all the aspects we would have liked to look at[4]. (The Appendix at the end of this book describes the different sources we have used – and the places where others who wish to find data on children may start their search.)

We consider four domains of welfare, or four key functionings that we believe a child needs to lead a 'good life' in Europe: material well-being, health and survival, education and personal development, and social inclusion/participation. These turn out to be – perhaps not surprisingly – the same domains as those covered by the *Human Development Report*'s index of deprivation in industrialised countries (UNDP, 1998). But the precise indicators we choose to capture elements of them differ from the UNDP indicators in several respects, reflecting both our different judgement of the suitable measures and the availability of time-series of data, as well as our focus on children. The four domains also reflect the concept of children's well-being and development in the UN Convention on the Rights of the Child.

The UN Convention defines a child as anyone under the age of 18 but this is not the age limit used in the definition of 'children' in many data sources. The cut-off varies considerably and is sometimes higher than 18 but is often lower. (The definition for older children can sometimes also include a criterion of study in full-time education.) This is an important practical consideration in the comparison of statistics across different indicators, or across different sources for the same indicator.

From a conceptual standpoint, the precise age cut-off is not that important. The key point is that 'childhood' covers several different stages of life and any choice of indicators of child welfare must reflect this. Some of our indicators refer to children of all ages taken together while others are specific to particular age groups. Several relate to older children, including young people over the age of 18. While discussion of child welfare in less-developed countries often focuses on younger children, the various pressures faced by teenagers in industrialised societies have been the subject of much investigation (for example Rutter and Smith, 1995). However, we do not attempt to analyse indicators for each of our domains for every stage of childhood systematically, and our analysis is inevitably somewhat eclectic as a result.

Despite the industrialised country setting, several of our indicators turned out to be more traditional at the end of the day than we had envisaged. For example, our indicator of health is restricted to mortality: hence we ignore the topical issues of sexually transmitted diseases and drug and alcohol abuse, as well as new illnesses affecting younger children in industrialised countries (such as the growing incidence of asthma). Our analysis of education focuses on expenditure and enrolment data, rather then learning achievement (although we shed some light on the variation in the latter across Europe at one point in time, together with its relationship with enrolment). Another gap is the lack of any analysis of children in institutions, both in prisons and in institutions of public care.

All these restrictions are to be regretted, but they are forced on us by the lack of available data. To take but one example, despite the enormous interest in the spread of sexually transmitted diseases that has, in part, been generated by the rise of HIV/AIDS, it seems that no data are readily available from any international organisation that gives the prevalence of the various diseases across the different European countries among the standard demographic group of 15-24 year olds[5]. Our conclusions at the end of this book include recommendations for further data collection so as to give a more complete picture of the well-being of Europe's children and how it is developing over time.

The indicators we are able to consider are listed below. Our choice of each is discussed in greater detail in the chapters that follow, but the domains in which indicators can be argued to fall are given in brackets (H = survival and health, E = education and development, M = material well-being, S = social inclusion). (In one or two cases the reasons for our classification may only become clear in later chapters.)

Economic well-being

- GDP per capita (M)
- Child poverty rate – children living in households with income below 50% of the national median (M, S)
- Prevalence of worklessness among households with children (M, S)
- Unemployment among all 20-24 year olds (M, S)

Mortality

- Under-5 and young persons' mortality (H)
- Death rate from motor vehicle accidents, 5-14 year olds (H, E)
- Suicide rate among young men aged 15-24 (H, S)

Education

- Percentage of 16 year olds in education (E)
- Expenditure on education as % of GDP, adjusted for age-structure (E)

Teenage fertility

- Birth rate to 15-19 year olds (E, S; perhaps also a risk factor for H, E, M, S)

Finally, we include one subjective indicator of well-being.

Life satisfaction

- Percentage of 15-19 year olds who classify themselves as 'satisfied' or 'very satisfied' with their life (H, E, M, S)

To give an initial idea of where European countries stand on these indicators, Table 2.1 presents the data for each for the most recent year available. (The full set of data used in the book are given in the Appendix tables.) The final line in the table shows the correlations with GDP per

Table 2.1: Indicators of child welfare in the EU

	Economic well-being				Mortality		
	GDP per capita (PPS) as % of EU average 1996	Children in poor households (%) 1993	Families with no working adult (%) 1996	Unemployment: % of all 20-24 year olds 1994	Under-5 mortality (deaths per 1,000) 1995	Traffic deaths all 5-14s (per 100,000) 1994	Male suicides 15-24 (per 100,000) 1994
Austria	107.5	–	4.9	–	6.7	3.4	26.5
Belgium	112.6	15	11.0	12.0	9.6	5.6	20.2
Denmark	115.2	5	–	9.7	6.3	4.4	15.9
Finland	93.1	–	11.8	19.6	5.0	4.7	50.5
France	106.4	12	8.8	14.4	7.1	3.4	23.5
Germany	108.3	13	8.6	6.5	7.1	3.2	16.5
Greece	64.9	19	4.5	15.3	9.0	4.7	4.2
Ireland	99.8	28	15.4	16.1	7.3	3.5	23.4
Italy	105.1	24	7.6	16.8	8.5	3.4	7.6
Luxembourg	168.9	23	3.8	4.3	4.4	4.3	28.0
Netherlands	104.7	16	9.3	7.6	6.8	3.7	9.9
Portugal	67.5	27	3.3	8.9	9.6	7.4	15.8
Spain	77.0	25	10.1	26.6	7.6	4.6	7.1
Sweden	97.2	–	–	10.9	4.7	1.9	15.7
UK	99.0	32	19.5	11.4	7.2	2.9	18.5
EU weighted average	100.0	20.4	10.5	13.8	7.5	3.6	15.2
max/min	2.6	6.4	5.8	6.1	2.2	3.9	12.0
correlation with GDP per capita	1.00	-0.28	-0.06	-0.56	-0.58	-0.26	0.31

Table 2.1: continued

	Education		Teen fertility	Happiness
	Education expenditure as % of GNP 1995	16 year old enrolment in education (%) 1994	Teenage fertility (births per 1,000) 1995	Life satisfaction, 15-19 year olds (%) 1990-94
Austria	5.7	90	17.5	–
Belgium	5.9	100	9.2	89.1
Denmark	8.7	92	8.7	97.9
Finland	7.7	92	9.8	–
France	5.5	92	9.6	85.5
Germany	5.3	96	13.0	87.8
Greece	3.5	79	12.9	74.7
Ireland	4.6	91	15.1	90.0
Italy	5.1	–	7.0	87.4
Luxembourg	–	77	10.6	97.0
Netherlands	5.3	89	5.8	98.6
Portugal	4.8	78	20.2	86.7
Spain	4.5	89	8.3	85.0
Sweden	8.3	95	8.6	–
UK	5.0	82	28.5	90.5
EU weighted average	5.2	90	10.7	87.7
max/min	2.5	1.3	4.9	1.3
correlation with GDP per capita	0.55	0.06	-0.26	0.63

Note: The weights used to calculate the means are described in the Appendix. Correlations with GDP per capita (in PPS) are for the year in question (1992 is taken in the case of satisfaction) and are unweighted for differences in population size.

Source: Appendix Tables A1, A2 (ECHP figures), A4, A5, B1, B3, B5, C2, C4, D1, E1

capita (in the relevant year), the focus of much earlier work on cohesion and the first of our indicators. While we would not necessarily expect to see any particular relationship between GDP per capita and some of the indicators (such as child poverty, for which we take a relative measure), others seem likely to be broadly linked to GDP, such as the under-5 mortality rate and the education indicators. Others, such as surviving the threat of traffic accidents, might even be inversely related to national income; while whether or not life satisfaction increases with income is an open question.

In fact, as the table shows, the link is not clear-cut in several cases, starting with the fact that the highest under-5 mortality rates are found in the countries with the second highest GDP per capita in the EU (Belgium) and the second lowest (Portugal). Only life satisfaction has a correlation with GDP per capita that exceeds 0.6 (we discuss in Chapter 7 whether there is any causal relationship). Most indicators have a correlation of 0.3 or less in absolute value. Dividing countries on the level of overall child welfare is also difficult. The Netherlands, Denmark and Sweden stand out as having excellent records on most indicators and Portugal does badly on many, but in general, countries have mixed reports. For instance, the UK has a very good road safety record but the highest rates of child poverty and of teenage fertility in the EU. Spain has the highest unemployment among 20-24 year olds but a low teen suicide rate; France has a relatively high suicide rate but a low poverty rate.

Measuring differences and convergence

While a static comparison of current national performance on these indicators is of interest, our focus in this book is on trends over time, in particular whether countries are becoming more similar in different dimensions on child well-being. Today's disparities could represent a mid-point on the path of movement of countries towards each other – or they could be points on divergent paths. Furthermore, all countries could be improving their performance in absolute terms, and yet still not be getting closer to eradicating cross-national differences.

Of course, convergence does not necessarily mean a movement towards the best performance; it could equally well be achieved by a general deterioration towards the standards of the worst. But as the *First report on economic and social cohesion* puts it: "Cohesion is concerned with ... new opportunities in the poorer regions and for disadvantaged social groups" (European Commission, 1996, p 14). Where cohesion is reached through a reduction of opportunities in areas initially better off, the report talks of 'negative convergence'. Naturally in this book we too are hoping to find 'positive' convergence, not convergence at any price. Where convergence represents a movement to reduced disparities around a lower average level of welfare we make sure to point this out – in this situation it would have been better had the member states remained as they were rather than converged.

How do we decide whether convergence has taken place? The literature on economic growth makes a distinction between two concepts: 'beta' convergence and 'sigma' convergence (see, for example, Sala-i-Martin, 1996a, 1996b). Beta convergence refers to the relationship between a country's initial performance and the change in its performance over time. If one country starts off with a poor record on a particular indicator but records good progress, while in another country that indicator starts off well but improves more slowly (or even declines), we have beta convergence between the two countries. In the case of the national incomes of a group of countries, there is said to be beta convergence if a negative relationship is found between the GDP growth rate and the initial level of income, with poorer countries growing more quickly.

Sigma convergence, on the other hand, refers to the change in the overall dispersion in the distribution. If the dispersion falls over time there is sigma convergence, irrespective of how particular countries are moving in the distribution. Sigma convergence is usually measured with the standard deviation of the log of income (for example DeLong, 1988; Sala-i-Martin, 1996b) but sometimes using the coefficient of variation – the standard deviation divided by the mean (for example Dowrick and Nguyen, 1989; Raiser, 1998). Occasional reference is also made to the ratio between maximum and minimum (for example Baumol, 1986).

Beta convergence is a necessary condition for sigma convergence – the overall dispersion cannot fall unless the countries with poorer records are moving towards those with better records[6]. But it is not a sufficient condition: countries which start off doing worst might surpass those initially doing better, leading to a changing of places in the distribution but no reduction (or even an increase) in the overall dispersion. In this book we are largely concerned with sigma convergence – the change in the 'spread' in the distribution – but the beta concept is useful in isolating what is driving this overall dispersion. For each indicator of welfare we pick out movements by individual countries and draw attention to changes in the rankings that occur, as well as reporting how the overall spread changes.

The coefficient of variation, the standard deviation of the log and the ratio between the maximum and minimum all describe the *relative* variation in the data. A conclusion about whether or not convergence is occurring will not depend on the absolute values in any year. This property of 'scale invariance' is typically sought in inequality measures by researchers working with data on incomes or expenditures. But what would the use of a scale invariant measure imply in this book, given our selected indicators of well-being?

Imagine that under-5 mortality in countries A and B is 100 deaths and 25 deaths respectively (per 1,000 live births) in 1960, but falls to values of 20 and 4 deaths in 1990. Should we conclude that infant mortality in these two countries has become more similar or less similar over time? The scale invariant measures would indicate divergence between the two countries, the ratio of maximum to minimum, for example, rising from 4 to 5. However, as an alternative, one might consider the *absolute* distance between the two countries, and reason that a difference of 16 deaths per 1,000 children compared to one of 75 deaths implies that the two countries had moved closer together.

This alternative approach, focusing on the absolute differences, has the advantage of giving a conclusion that is robust to what might at first seem an innocuous change in the way we look at the data. Unlike income and expenditure, many of our indicators have a natural 'dual' or complement: survival instead of mortality, and employment rather than unemployment. This dual is obtained trivially by a simple transformation of the data – survival is what is 'left over' after mortality, and the under-5 child survival rate is simply 1,000 minus the under-5 mortality rate (hence the label 'complement' in the mathematical sense). Unless there is a good argument for looking at the data in one way rather than the other, we need to be sure that our conclusions concerning convergence do not depend on the choice we make[7].

Use of the scale invariant measures does not guarantee this. In the example just given of child mortality, the survival rates would be 900 and 975 in 1960 and 980 and 994 in 1990, and the ratio of maximum to minimum *falls* over time, from 1.083 to 1.014. The conclusion about convergence in this example is sensitive to the way the data are presented. The alternative approach based on absolute differences gives exactly the same answer in both cases – that inequality fell[8].

The standard deviation is based on absolute differences and is therefore unchanged by the switch from mortality to survival or between any other pair of complementary indicators – conclusions about convergence will hence be robust to the choice over the way in which to present the data. This advantage in terms of robustness comes at a price: one has to accept a view of inequality based on absolute rather than relative differences. But the attraction of obtaining a robust result is clearly large and we therefore take the standard deviation as our principal measure of dispersion. We include, however, the coefficient of variation and the ratio of maximum to minimum among the summary statistics in the tables in the Appendix, and in presenting our findings we note when these scale invariant measures lead to different conclusions[9].

An important issue that arises in calculating the degree of variation across member states in any indicator is whether to take into account the greatly varying populations of the different countries. Germany has a population of 82 million people; Luxembourg has just 400,000. Three other countries have populations of over 55 million; eight others have 10 million or less. Should one let the figure for Luxembourg have equal weight in the calculations with that for Germany? Or should one let the German figure be 200 times more important?

The answer to this question depends on what one is trying to measure. Suppose that we are concerned with the full extent of the variation in an indicator across the entire population of the EU, for example poverty risk or satisfaction level. The total variance can be decomposed into the variation within member states and that between them. The latter may be calculated from the average values of the indicator concerned for each country – the average poverty rate, the proportion of persons satisfied with their lives, and so on. The formula for this between-group element of the total variation does indeed weight the contribution of each country according to its population. Greece should get a weight that is twice that of Denmark and nearly three times that of Ireland. Luxembourg should not get an equal weight in the calculation to that of Germany. In this case our interest is in the variation across member states because it is one part of the total variation across the European population. In general, a reduction over time in this between-group variation – 'convergence' – is in fact neither a necessary nor a sufficient condition for a reduction in disparities across the European population as a whole, since changes in the differences within countries have to be considered as well. Nevertheless, change in the between-group variation is certainly one influence on the total variation[10].

On the other hand, we may not be concerned with variation across the EU population as a whole but rather with the variation across the countries themselves, viewed as separate entities. The principle of 'subsidiarity' implies that it is the member states that will have the responsibility for policy within the Union whenever possible. Imagine we want a measure of variation in child welfare that shows when one country is out of line with the others, signalling the need for possible action by the member state concerned. In this case the different sizes of the countries is irrelevant and we certainly would not want the calculation to be dominated by the large countries. For this reason we think that both unweighted as well as weighted calculations are of interest and we present both in the Appendix, pointing out in the text when they tell a different story[11]. Unless otherwise noted, however, the figures we present for both the mean and standard deviation are the weighted ones.

Finally, there is the issue of the time-period in which we are interested. The book has a dual focus. On the one hand, we are interested in the issue of long-run cohesion in Europe; we consider whether or not child well-being has been converging in the last 25 years. We are able for some indicators to put this into the context of a longer period, while for others the available time-series are shorter. On the other hand, we are also interested in the immediate term: has child welfare been converging in the 1990s, during the run-up to monetary union itself, or have the patterns across countries been moving in a different way to those for the macroeconomic indicators? Unfortunately, a lack of data means that for many indicators we cannot explore this fully. For instance, did the tight terms of the Maastricht Treaty lead to an increase in child poverty in countries working hard to meet the criteria for membership of the single currency? This is not a question we can answer with the published data for child poverty shown in Table 2.1, which end in 1993. But where possible we ask whether the 1990s give us evidence of a different trend to that observed in the previous two decades.

Notes

[1] For a discussion of the Jerusalem Initiative, see also Adamson (1996), writing in the UNICEF publication *The progress of nations*, which has a section each year containing indicators of child well-being in industrialised countries.

[2] The USA has a rich stream of data on child well-being at both federal and state level. An excellent publication at the federal level is *America's children: Key national indicators of well-being, 1998* (Federal Interagency Forum on Child and Family Statistics, 1998). An example at the state level is the 'Kids Count' analyses of the Annie E. Casey Foundation (www.aecf.org). Collection of

data and analysis at the state level have been spurred on in recent years by reform of federal cash transfers to families ('welfare reform'). At the same time, the particular institutional setting of the USA results in use of some indicators that would not necessarily be relevant in Europe. For example, an important indicator in the National Survey of America's Families, which forms part of the Urban Institute's project on 'Assessing the New Federalism', is the coverage of children by health insurance (see www.urban.org).

[3] For example, *A social portrait of Europe* (Eurostat, 1996) provides an excellent overview of living and working conditions in the 15 member states, but contains little information on the situation of children (especially young children). Further data on specific issues are available in *Youth in the European Union* (Eurostat, 1997a), *Key data on education in the European Union* (Eurostat, 1997b), and the annual *Demographic Statistics* and *Eurostat Yearbook* (for example Eurostat, 1990 and 1997d).

[4] Use of national statistical offices or of a network of national informants might have extended the possibilities open to us considerably, but for practical reasons we rely entirely on existing cross-national collections of data.

[5] This is not to say that the data do not exist; it is simply that they do not appear to be readily available on a cross-national basis from a single source. (This is a good example of a subject where a network of national informants might have been able to provide us with the necessary information.)

[6] Assume that the log of income in one period is expressed as the sum of a fraction, b, of its value in the previous period, a constant term, and a random element. Strictly speaking, the condition for beta convergence to be necessary for sigma convergence requires not only that $b<1$ but also that the random element has a constant variance and is independent across both time and countries.

[7] The analogy with income or expenditure is in fact better with the dual concept – 'more' representing a higher level of welfare – although this does not seem a particularly strong argument.

[8] A switch to the dual concept does not *necessarily* overturn the conclusion about convergence based on a scale invariant measure. For example, in the example of the two countries' mortality rates considered in the text, imagine that country B had an mortality rate of 6 in 1990 rather than 4. In this case

the ratio of maximum to minimum would have fallen for the mortality rate as well as for the survival rate.

[9] It is important to distinguish the issue of relative versus absolute differences from another one which arises when large changes occur over time in the average value of an indicator, as in the example given in the text of child mortality. In this case it may be difficult to separate in one's mind the concept of 'pure inequality' from a measure of welfare that incorporates the average value as well as the degree of dispersion. (In the terminology of the economic measurement of welfare, people may think in Generalised Lorenz and not Lorenz terms.)

[10] Suppose that the value of the indicator for any person in a given country is made up of a country-specific constant, equal for all persons in that country, plus an element that differs from person to person, the value of which is distributed randomly across the country's population. Suppose the variance of the latter is constant over time in each country – the within-group variation is unchanged – and that the relative populations of the countries are constant. In this case the changes in the total variation in the indicator over time across the EU population are driven entirely by the changes in the country-specific constants, summarised by the between-group variation.

[11] The weights used depend on the indicator in question, for example the child population in each country is taken for indicators relating to all children, the teenage populations for teenage indicators and so on. The *First report on economic and social cohesion* does not explicitly discuss the issues of scale invariance or weighting (European Commission, 1996). In general, scale invariant measures were used together with weighting by population size.

THREE

Economic well-being

To argue that child welfare goes well beyond consideration of national income is not to deny the importance to children of the economic strength of the countries in which they live. We therefore start this chapter by looking briefly at the indicator that has been the focus of much earlier work on convergence of living standards in the EU, GDP per capita. If national incomes are converging sufficiently strongly, then differences among member states in at least some aspects of the economic well-being of children and their families should be narrowing.

Figure 3.1 summarises the change in disparities of GDP per capita since the early 1980s, measured in purchasing power standard (PPS) terms[1]. (We follow the example of the *First report on economic and social cohesion* [European Commission, 1996] and do not consider earlier periods.) In this instance we do measure disparities using scale invariant indicators – measures of relative rather than absolute differences – that are standard in the literature on convergence across countries in national incomes.

Between 1983 and 1996, real GDP per capita in the EU 15 rose by about a third. A substantial reduction in relative disparities in national incomes took place during this period up until the early 1990s, the weighted coefficient of variation falling by a quarter between 1983 and 1993. The unweighted figure on the other hand (not shown in the diagram) was unchanged on account of a sharp rise in income in what is both the richest and the smallest country, Luxembourg, where income per head rose to about two thirds above the EU average (with the effect also of increasing the ratio of the maximum to the minimum).

The convergence in the weighted data was associated in part with faster growth by the Cohesion Four – Ireland, Greece, Portugal, Spain – which are shown in Figure 3.1 as moving up relative to other member states. (By contrast, the absolute difference in real incomes between the Cohesion Four and the other 11 member states was broadly the same in 1983 and 1996.) The situation, however, varied substantially among these four countries. While Irish income per head rose from 64% to

Figure 3.1: Disparities in national income (GDP per capita in PPS)

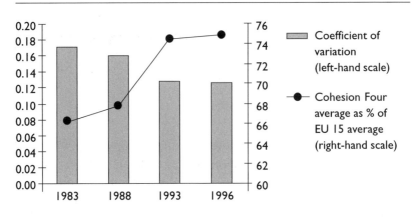

Source: Table A1

83% of the EU average over 1983-93, the Greek figure increased from 62% to only 65%. (Greece slipped behind Portugal in 1989 to become the country with the lowest GDP per capita.) The 1990s, however, have seen little or no continuation of the trend towards convergence (at least in the period up to 1996). Among the Cohesion Four, only in Ireland has catch-up growth continued – in fact, here GDP per capita in 1996 was at exactly the Union average.

GDP per capita is, of course, a very crude proxy for average incomes of families with children, especially in those member states where the proportion of households with children is relatively low. It does have the advantage of including government expenditure on basic social services, such as education and health, which provide important non-cash income to families. (We return in Chapter 5 to the issue of public expenditure on education.) But this aside, any serious analysis of trends in average incomes of families in the EU would need an indicator more directly related to the household sector, and, within that sector, to children[2].

An analysis of average incomes of families would, however, refer to just that, *average* incomes, ignoring the variation in family incomes within each member state. Our principal concern in this chapter is with children at the margins of society in the Union. We first consider child poverty, on which the distribution of income within each country has a direct bearing. We then address a related issue, but one also important in its own right, that of children living in households with no adult in work.

Finally, we look at disparities across the EU in the unemployment of young persons themselves.

Child poverty

Much more information on poverty in Europe is now available than was the case in the mid-1980s (Atkinson, 1995, 1998b). There are more national studies, and at the European level there have been several important initiatives, including the work by Hagenaars et al (1994) for the late 1980s based on existing national data sets. Hagenaars and her colleagues covered all the then EU 12 and included figures for child as well as overall poverty. The European Community Household Panel (ECHP), sponsored by Eurostat, is a major development in terms of data (Eurostat, 1997e, 1999). The figures for child poverty in 1993 shown in Table 2.1 are taken from Eurostat's own analysis of Wave 1 of ECHP, and as further waves become available ECHP could provide considerable additional insight into how family incomes have changed in the 1990s during the run-up to monetary union.

The ECHP figures refer to the proportion of children living in households with incomes below 50% of the average income in their own countries. This is a measure of *relative* poverty, implementing the EU's broad definition of poverty as persons with "resources (material, cultural and social) that are so limited as to exclude them from the minimum acceptable way of life in the Member States in which they live" (Eurostat, 1997e, p 3). The figures, which refer to the EU 12, vary widely, with as few as 5% of children classified in poverty in Denmark and as many as 32% in the UK. It is notable that three of the worst performers are the cohesion countries of Spain, Portugal and Ireland, countries where income inequality is comparatively high.

Poverty figures from Wave 1 of the ECHP have been the subject of considerable attention, not least since they give a different picture in some respects to earlier analyses, stimulating debate as to whether this is due to the differences in the nature of the sources. In Table A2 in the Appendix we give the ECHP figures for child poverty together with those from Hagenaars et al (1994) and from the source we use to look at changes over time, Bradbury and Jäntti (1999). The reader should note the differences in methodology and coverage shown at the top of each column of results; these notwithstanding, the comparison raises questions in particular about the position in the Benelux countries shown by the ECHP data[3].

Has the degree of exclusion of children, as measured by relative poverty, become more or less equal across the Union over time? Convergence of average income per head shown in Figure 3.1 has no direct bearing on this question – the answer depends on (i) changes in the distribution of income within each country and (ii) changes in the position of families with children in those national distributions[4]. Our ability to provide the answer is limited by available analyses of the existing data. While subsequent waves of ECHP should shed light on the situation during the 1990s, the trends prior to the 1990s are harder to establish. The availability of data differs across countries, the data and methods are not always sufficiently comparable, and results do not always separately identify children.

Our results refer only to nine countries and cover just the period between the mid-1980s and the early 1990s. The source is the analysis of child poverty by Bradbury and Jäntti (1999) which uses the household survey data sets held in the Luxembourg Income Study (LIS). The data sets available in the LIS certainly do differ but have been harmonised to make them sufficiently comparable at a broad level across country as well as across time. And the treatment of the data by the authors – the method used to calculate poverty – is the same in each case. (The differences in methodology shown in Table A2 between the different studies are a reminder of the need for such standardisation.) Figure 3.2 shows child poverty rates based on a poverty line of 50% of the median national income. This contrasts with the figures from the ECHP in Table 2.1 in which the poverty line is based on the *mean*, which results in higher numbers in poverty, although other differences in the treatment of the data and in the nature of the data sets also affect the comparison.

These data show a rise in child poverty in the nine member states concerned, taken together, from 10.5% to 13.5%. Only in Finland and Sweden, countries with below average poverty in the 1980s, is any real fall recorded. Large rises occur in the two countries with the highest rates in the 1980s: Germany – four percentage points over a 10-year period, and Britain – six percentage points over a five-year period. (It should be noted that the German data for the 1990s include former East Germany.) This pattern of changes drives up the dispersion in poverty rates across the countries concerned. If data for France for 1981 and 1989 and for Spain for 1980 and 1990 are also included (treating 1989 in the former case as '1990s'), the picture is more or less unchanged – the same story emerges concerning the overall levels of child poverty, the dispersion across countries and the changes in both of these over time. Several member states are absent from this analysis, notably three of the Cohesion Four, and it would be particularly interesting to see the

Figure 3.2: Child poverty in the 1980s and the 1990s (%)

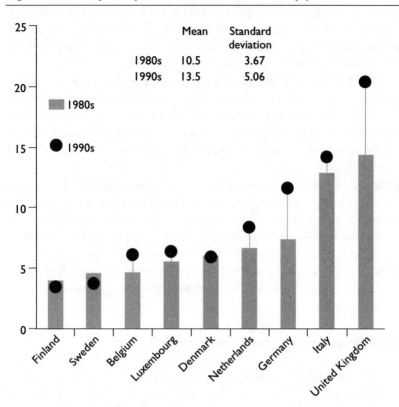

Note: A child is defined as in poverty if equivalised household income is less than 50% of the national median. The notes to Table A2 give the equivalence scale used and Table A3 gives the years to which the data refer. Children are defined as all persons aged 0-17.

Source: Table A3

trends in child poverty in these countries. Among countries for which data are available, however, the conclusion seems to be that disparities among member states rose between the mid-1980s and the early 1990s against a background of an increasing average level[5].

This conclusion of course relates to a particular measure of poverty: one that takes no account of differences in average national incomes. A child in Spain is classified as poor solely on the basis of a comparison of his or her household's income with the Spanish median. But it may be argued that poverty measurement within the EU *should* take account of living standards in the Union as a whole, reflecting the notion of social cohesion among member states[6]. Countries with lower average incomes would then record higher poverty rates for a given distribution of income. And catch-up with the rest of the EU by the Cohesion Four in terms of national income per head would have the effect of reducing poverty in those countries, other factors remaining unchanged.

Whether this in turn would lead to reduced dispersion in poverty rates across the Union would depend on each cohesion country's point of departure compared to those of other member states, which depends on the distribution of income as well as on average income, but the likelihood is that this reduction would occur. However, changes in the distribution of income within countries, and any alterations in the position of families with children within these distributions, would remain critical, something true of all members states and not just the Cohesion Four. These may greatly moderate the impact of economic growth on poverty when the latter is assessed using an absolute yardstick. Measuring poverty using the official US poverty line in constant price terms, child poverty in the UK is estimated to have fallen by less than 2 percentage points between 1986 and 1995, despite growth in real GDP per capita of 20%[7].

Children in workless households

One dimension of children's economic well-being is the strength of their households' contact with the labour market. This has an important effect on the risk of being poor. In the late 1980s, children aged under 14 in EU households with no working adult were on average four times more likely to be in poverty than were children in households in which someone worked (Hagenaars et al, 1994, Appendix 3, Table A3.1), although this figure varied substantially from country to country. On the other hand, a feature of the rise in unemployment in Europe since the late 1970s has been the lack of a clear link in a number of countries between the changes in unemployment and the changes in poverty among the population as a whole (Atkinson, 1998c).

But it is not just the impact on poverty that is of concern. Households without work are more precarious than are other households, with a greater need for income support from the state. Other aspects of worklessness go beyond the economic dimension. The lack of work in a household may cause tension within the family and may limit a child's aspirations and contacts. For these different reasons, the proportion of children living in households without work may be taken as one measure of economic and social exclusion[8].

The analysis of workless households in Europe has been advanced by Gregg and Wadsworth's investigation of whether there has been growing 'polarisation' in OECD countries – a simultaneous rise in the number of households with *all* adults present in employment and in the number with *no* adult employed (Gregg and Wadsworth, 1996). The picture appears to vary between countries, with some displaying polarisation and some not. But the debate has not tended to focus on the situation of children – on the changing proportion of children who live in workless households in different countries[9]. However, recent work on workless households by the OECD provides an important source of information that we draw on here.

Figure 3.3 shows for 11 EU countries the percentage of working-age households containing one or more children aged under 15 that had no working-age adult in employment. The data refer to 1985 and 1996, years in which the (unweighted) average unemployment rate for the countries concerned was the same. The unit of analysis is the household and not the child; unfortunately the data do not show the percentage of children living in households where no adult is in work, which is the figure of more interest from a child welfare perspective. Data for two further countries, Austria and Finland, are given for 1996 in Table 2.1. (The only countries for which no data are available are Denmark and Sweden.)

The incidence of worklessness among households with children clearly varies substantially across the EU. The figure in 1996 ranges from less than 4% in Portugal and Luxembourg to 15% in Ireland and almost 20% in the UK. The value of the standard deviation shows disparities to have risen somewhat since 1985. Moreover, this increase in dispersion went hand-in-hand with a higher overall rate of joblessness – the weighted average for the EU 11 rose by over 2 percentage points over the period concerned, despite the unemployment rate showing little change.

What lies behind the figures? Polarisation of work along the lines suggested by Gregg and Wadsworth could result in higher worklessness among families even if overall conditions in the labour market are unchanged. Figure 3.4 plots the change in worklessness among households with children against changes in the unemployment rate. Although a number of countries lie close to the 45 degree line, in several the change in unemployment is a poor guide to the change in worklessness. In Greece, Belgium and the UK the changes have been in opposite directions.

Figure 3.3: Households with children that have no working adult (%)

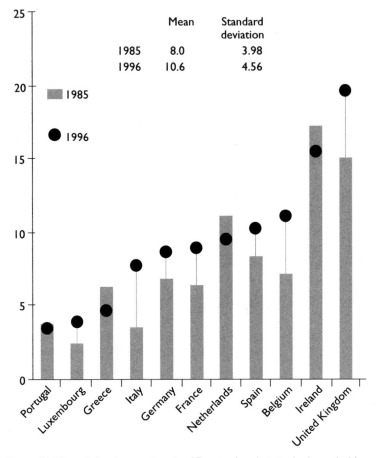

Note: Children defined as aged under 15; unit of analysis is the household.

Source: Table A4

The case of the UK stands out. This is underlined by the contrast with the situation of Portugal. The two countries had the same labour force participation rate in 1996 for 25-54 year olds (83%) and very similar unemployment rates (6.2% and 7.0%, respectively, for the same age group)[10]. And yet there is a 16 percentage point gap between these two countries in the proportion of households with children with an adult in work.

The association across countries at any one point in time between labour market conditions and worklessness among families is, not surprisingly, quite strong in general. But this association is moderated by the big differences that exist in household structure, in particular in the *number* of working-age adults present in households with children. In Portugal less than 5% of households with children have only one working-age adult – something true also of the other Southern European countries, Greece, Italy and Spain. By contrast, the figure is 10% or more in Austria, Finland, France and Germany, and as much as 18% in the UK. Single-adult households are far less likely to have work than are other households with children – averaging across all EU countries for which there are data, 40% and 6% respectively of these two types of household had no adult in work in 1996[11]. All the Southern European countries have a 'workless family' rate below the unemployment rate for 25-54 year olds, while the opposite is true in Belgium, Germany, Ireland, Luxembourg, the Netherlands and the UK.

Figure 3.4: Change in worklessness among families and change in unemployment (1985-96)

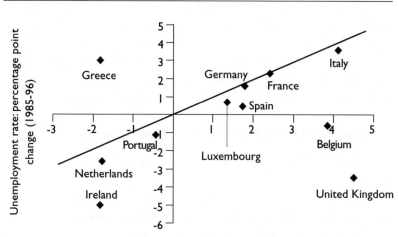

No adult working rate: percentage point change (1985-96)

Note: The unemployment rate is the economy-wide figure for all 25-54 year olds while the no adult working rate refers to households with children (aged under 15). The diagram shows the percentage point changes in each of these rates over 1985-96.

Source: Workless household rates, from Table A4; unemployment rates are OECD standardised rates, which are benchmarked to labour force survey estimates, and are from Eurostat (1997d, p 304) and OECD (1990, p 36) (with the exception of the 1996 figure for Germany which is taken from OECD (1998, p 190). The 1985 rates, which were taken from the latter source, were adjusted by the ratio of figures for 1986 given in both sources.

The differences in household structure can be expected to affect the impact of the economic cycle on the overall level of worklessness among families, together with the dispersion in levels across member states. But household structure itself changes over time. And in contrast to the economy, these changes represent trends rather than cycles, producing more lasting effects on worklessness. All countries featured in Figures 3.3 and 3.4 experienced an increase in the importance of one-adult households with children between 1985 and 1996, reflecting in part a rise in births to lone parents and in divorce. However, the extent of this increase varies markedly. In seven countries the rise in the share of single-adult households among all households with children was 2 percentage points or less. In France it was 3 points, in Belgium and Ireland 4-5 points, while in the UK it was over 10 points. It is this large rise that drives the change in the overall worklessness rate for UK families[12].

Patterns of worklessness for families in the EU, including the extent of differences among member states, therefore depend on a variety of factors – the economic cycle, polarisation in the labour market, and changing household structure. If household structure in Southern Europe moves towards that in Northern Europe then further convergence in household worklessness at a higher overall rate could be the outcome, although the future is of course hard to predict.

Unemployment among young people

For older children, concern about the impact of the labour market on well-being must include consideration of their own employment opportunities. Rather than looking at the teenage years we focus on unemployment rates among those aged 20-24. A concern with child welfare extends beyond the years up to the age of 18 – looking at the prospects for children when they pass over the age of majority is essential for any rounded picture of their well-being[13].

The high rates of youth unemployment in much of the EU are a disappointing feature of labour markets in many member states. Unemployment rates among 20-24 year olds exceeded 20% in seven out of 14 countries in 1994 (we have no data for Austria). Spain tops the league at over 40%.

These rates refer to unemployment among young people who have joined the labour market, that is, among those who are part of the labour force. But labour force participation rates among the young differ substantially across the Union, driven in large measure by differences in enrolment rates in full-time education. Whereas over 75% of 20-24 year olds in Denmark and the UK were in the labour force in 1994, the figure was less than 55% in France and Italy. There is also a reasonably clear association between participation in the labour market and unemployment, as shown by Figure 3.5. Participation is lower where the risk of unemployment is higher. One result is that the variation across the EU member states in the proportion of *all* young persons aged 20-24 who are unemployed is somewhat less than that among those who are part of the labour force.

Figure 3.5: Labour force participation and employment, 20-24 year olds (1994)

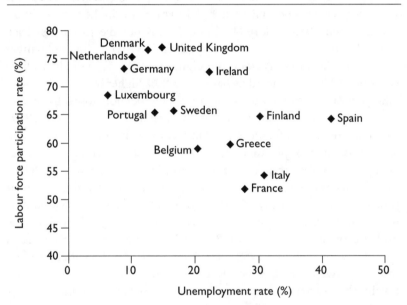

Note: Unemployment follows the International Labour Organisation (ILO)/OECD definition and the rates displayed refer to those young people who are in the labour force.

Source: Tables A5 and A6

Our interest in unemployment is as an inverse measure of well-being among young people, as opposed to a measure of disequilibrium in the youth labour market. It is thus the incidence among the full age cohort that is arguably of most interest. Hence in looking at trends over time we remove the influence of differences – and changes – in labour force participation and calculate unemployment rates as a percentage of all persons aged 20-24[14].

Figure 3.6 shows the unemployment rate for 20-24 year olds on this basis for 1979 and 1994, and for two intervening years. The rates for just seven countries are shown, but the weighted EU mean and standard deviation are reported in Table 3.1 for 14 countries (Austria is the country not included) for 1983-94 and for 1979-94 for the eight countries for which we have data for all four years. (Ireland is the country excluded from Figure 3.6.) Following the rise in unemployment in the early 1980s, the EU 8 mean changes little over 1983-94. The EU 14 figure shows nearly one in seven of the age group unemployed in 1994.

How have differences in the risk of unemployment among member states varied over time? The standard deviation for the 14 rose by almost half between 1983 and 1994, although it is notable that it fell back somewhat in the five years from its peak in 1989 when unemployment was at a cyclical low. Among the eight countries for which we have data since 1979 the standard deviation was 80% higher by 1994. Absolute differences among this group of member states therefore rose substantially. Exactly the same percentage increase occurred in the mean over 1979-94, hence relative differences were in fact unchanged.

The rise in unemployment over 1979-94 saw the countries' rankings change in several respects. For example, the experiences of the neighbours Spain and Portugal, which started the period in a similar position, contrast sharply. A 20-24 year old in Spain was two-and-a-half times as likely to be unemployed in 1994 as in 1979, while the probability fell over time in Portugal. There were sharp rises in unemployment between 1989 and 1994 in two countries with previously low rates, Sweden and, especially, Finland, where the early 1990s saw a notable shrinkage in the economy on account of fall-out from the break-up of the former Soviet Union. Germany and the UK, however, are among the countries where unemployment fell between these two years.

Table 3.1: Cohort unemployment rate, 20-24 year olds:
summary statistics

		1979	1983	1989	1994
EU 8	Mean	8.3	13.9	13.6	14.8
	Standard deviation	3.8	4.7	7.1	6.8
EU 14	Mean	-	14.0	12.4	13.8
	Standard deviation	-	4.2	6.4	6.1

Note: The EU 8 are Finland, France, Germany, Ireland, Italy, Portugal, Spain and Sweden. Austria is the country missing from the EU 14. Unemployment rates are calculated as a percentage of all persons aged 20-24 and not just those participating in the labour force.

Source: Table A7

Figure 3.6: Cohort unemployment rate, 20-24 year olds (1979-94)

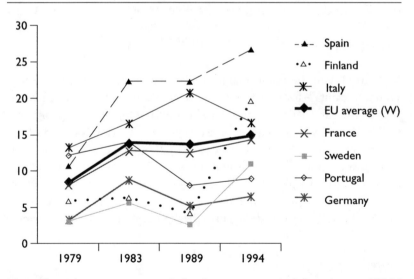

Note: Unemployment rates are calculated as a percentage of *all* persons aged 20-24 and not just those participating in the labour force.

Source: Table A7

Unemployment may reduce the welfare of young people in various ways, including a direct impact on incomes, wastage of their talents, and a feeling of exclusion from society. The impact on living standards will depend on the types of households in which young unemployed people live. Those that live in households where others are employed will be cushioned from part of the impact. But many young unemployed live in households where *no other adult works*, a fact that is often overlooked. In 1996, this applied to 40% of the unemployed aged 15-24 in four out of 12 member states for which data were available. The unweighted average figure across all 12 countries was 32% (OECD, 1998, Table 1.5). Among the lowest figures (but still over 20%) were those for Spain, Italy, and Greece – countries with high unemployment rates among the young. The lowest of all was that for Portugal; it is only here that less than one in five of unemployed 15-24 year olds were living in workless households.

These differences across the EU reflect a number of factors, one of which is the variation in household structure between Northern and Southern Europe, with young people staying on for longer in the parental home in the South[15]. The result is an evening out in the disparities in one dimension of the impact of unemployment on the young.

Summary

We started with the traditional indicator of average income per head – GDP per capita – for which relative disparities are now significantly less than in the early 1980s, against a background of higher average income in the EU as a whole. This contrasts with the situation for each of the other indicators we have considered in this chapter: child poverty, worklessness among households with children, and unemployment among young people. In each case, the disparities among countries (measured in absolute rather than relative terms) have tended to rise over the period considered – against a background of a worsening average for the EU as a whole.

Notes

[1] In the case of countries such as Ireland and Luxembourg, where foreign firms are a very prominent part of the economy, GNP per capita (which excludes repatriated profit and includes remittances from abroad) might be considered a more appropriate measure of average income.

[2] Vijay Verma of the University of Essex kindly provided us with information on mean equivalised household cash income per child in 10 EU countries in

1993 from the ECHP (see next section). (The countries are those for which there are poverty rates in Table 2.1, excluding Germany.) After converting the means to PPS terms, the weighted coefficient of variation is 0.163, which may be compared to that for GDP per capita for these countries in 1993 of 0.143. The weighted correlation between the two is only 0.78. (The unweighted correlation is much higher, 0.96, due to the greater influence of the high-income outlier, Luxembourg.)

[3] Callan and Nolan (1997) compare the poverty rates for all individuals in ECHP (not just children) with those of Hagenaars et al (1994), having put the data onto the same basis (in terms of the measure of resources taken, the poverty line and so on). (This contrasts with our Table A2, where the differences in methodology remain.) They comment that the size of the apparent rise in poverty indicated by the comparison between the late 1980s and 1993 "would indeed be remarkable" (p 64) for such a relatively short period and the implication is that some caution with ECHP data is needed.

[4] A crude argument based on the Kuznets curve would provide a link between, on the one hand, convergence in average incomes as a result of catch-up growth by the poorer countries and, on the other, a reduction in income inequality within these countries leading to convergence in relative poverty rates. We do not enter into the merits of such an argument here.

[5] These results seem consistent with the conclusion of Atkinson et al (1995) that continuing progression towards reduced income inequality in Europe was the exception in the 1980s rather than the rule.

[6] Another possibility suggested by Atkinson (1995, 1998b) is for a poverty line that is a weighted average of the EU and national averages. This would reflect both differences in the levels of development across the Union as well as the notion of social cohesion.

[7] We are grateful to Markus Jäntti for this calculation made using LIS data (other definitions are as those in Table A3).

[8] This is not to say that lack of work should be viewed as a bad thing in every case, and the extra time that parents without work may spend with children may of course be beneficial. The quality of jobs done by parents is also important from the child's point of view, including the number of hours worked and the degree of mental and physical stress.

[9] In the case of the USA, the annual government publication *Trends in the well-being of America's children and youth* gives the proportion of children with both resident parents (or the only resident parent) in the work force, which rose from 53% in 1980 to 66% in 1994 (DHHS, 1996, Table ES 3.1). But the numbers *without* any resident parent in the labour force are not given.

[10] These figures for unemployment and labour force participation are taken from OECD (1998, pp 195-6).

[11] It should be noted, however, that there are large differences in the rate of worklessness even when holding this aspect of household structure constant. Over 60% of single-adult households with children have no work in Ireland and the UK, compared with only 25% in Spain, Portugal and Austria.

[12] The rate of worklessness in fact fell slightly in one-adult households in the UK – as for other household types – but the shift in the distribution towards this high risk group pushed up the overall rate.

[13] There are also data problems with looking at unemployment for a younger age group using official register data: in some countries young people do not qualify for unemployment benefit until they are 18, making cross-country comparison of unemployment among 15-19 year olds based on register data misleading. The data we use are drawn, however, from labour force surveys in which the measurement of unemployment does not depend on registration for benefits.

[14] Tables A5 and A6 in the Appendix give the unemployment rate with the conventional denominator and the participation rate for several years; the (unweighted) average EU 14 participation rate fell by over 8 percentage points between 1983 and 1994 while unemployment rose by 3 points.

[15] The proportion of 20-24 year olds still living with their parents in 1995 was in the range 47-55% in France, Germany, the Netherlands, and the UK in 1994, but over 70% in Greece, and over 85% in Italy and Spain (Eurostat, 1997a, p 63).

FOUR

Mortality

Mortality indicators have become widely accepted as key non-economic measures of a population's well-being. Sen (1998) gives three reasons for their worth. First, of course, we attach intrinsic importance to life itself. Second, many other capabilities that we value are contingent on our being alive; and third, mortality is correlated with and therefore a rough proxy for a number of other dimensions of well-being for which data are less readily available – most obviously morbidity. Underlining all is the fact that mortality is not as easily explained by national wealth as might be expected. Although GDP is broadly correlated with both infant mortality (IMR) and life expectancy if countries at all income levels are included, over groups of countries with similar GDP wide disparities in mortality exist. This seems to be because traditional mortality indicators respond well to investment in basic public services and to the raising of the incomes of the poor, and because increasing national wealth is neither a necessary nor a sufficient condition for these improvements (see Anand and Ravallion, 1993).

Traditional mortality indicators

At very high levels of national income, however, we would expect disparities in traditional mortality indicators to have been more or less eliminated. Indeed, in Europe today no country has an IMR higher than nine deaths per 1,000 live births, and while disparities do persist they are negligible in the light of those in the past: in 1960 the IMR varied across Europe from 16 in Sweden to 81 in Portugal – the latter figure, for comparison, is higher than that for the Sudan in 1996 (UNICEF, 1998, Table 1). Similar progress has been achieved in the wider measure of under-5 mortality, as illustrated in Figure 4.1. The overall EU 15 rate fell by more than two thirds over 1970-95 – see Table 4.1. There is also clear evidence of convergence, with the standard deviation falling by some 90%[1]. As the bulk of child mortality in any one year is made up of deaths to the under-5s, this progress has in turn meant similar convergence in the mortality of all those under 18[2]. Death rates for boys and girls under 20 are about one third of what they were in 1970.

However, this progress does not mean that mortality data are no longer useful as measures of child well-being in the industrialised world. First, despite achievements, there are still unnecessary deaths. Imagine that all EU countries had the same under-5 mortality rate as that of Sweden. There would have been over 10,000 fewer deaths among the under-5s in 1995[3]. Second, given that deaths among young children dominate the total for children of all ages, improvements in the survival rates of very young children may disguise what is happening among other under-20s.

Figure 4.1: Under-5 mortality rates in selected EU countries (1970-95)

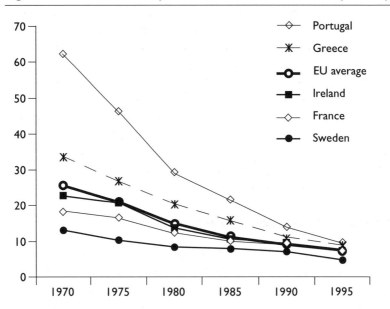

Note: The under-5 mortality rate gives the probability of dying before reaching the age of five, expressed per 1,000 births.

Source: Table B1

Indeed, when we look at older groups of children, we find progress has been more limited. Table 4.1 shows summary statistics for mortality rates among two older age groups alongside those for the under-5s. Among 5-14 year olds, death rates have been falling steadily since 1970, but much more slowly than for the under-5s. As a result, the standard deviation has also fallen much more slowly – starting off below that for under-5 mortality, it finishes much above it. Among 15-24 year olds the overall European mortality rate has fallen by only a quarter and with almost no progress over the last decade, while the standard deviation has come down by a little under half. In both cases, *relative* disparities have not improved at all: the coefficient of variation for both 5–14s and 15–24s has been more or less constant across the period[4].

Table 4.1: Mortality rates among three age groups of children, EU 15

		1970	1975	1980	1985	1990	1995
Mean	Under-5	25.8	20.8	14.9	11.3	9.2	7.5
	5-14	40.7	34.1	29.9	22.6	20.1	17.6
	15-24	88.5	84.9	80.2	67.7	69.6	65.0
Standard	Under-5	8.9	6.0	3.6	2.3	1.1	0.9
deviation	5-14	7.3	5.8	5.4	4.1	4.0	3.3
	15-24	18.8	18.3	16.6	12.7	12.5	11.3

Note: Both means and standard deviations are weighted figures. The under-5 mortality rate measures the probability of dying before the 5th birthday expressed per 1,000 live births. The mortality rates for 5-14 and for 15-24 year olds measure the total deaths among persons of these ages per 100,000 in the age group.

Source: Tables B1 and B2

Figure 4.2 presents trends in the death rate for the oldest age group for selected countries. A varied picture appears and it is clear that there has been some notable re-ranking within the league table. In the Southern European Cohesion countries and in Italy, death rates were as high for this group in 1995 as they had been in the early or mid-1970s. In Greece and Italy, for example, mortality rates started in 1970 at very similar levels to those in the Netherlands, but by 1995 the rates in both countries were nearly 50% higher than the Dutch rate. Portugal experiences a similar divergence from the EU average. At the same time, rapid progress has been made in the three countries which started with the highest youth mortality rates: Austria, Germany and Luxembourg (not shown). (German data to 1985 are for the Federal Republic only and from 1990 for the united Germany: the higher death rates in the former East Germany are reflected by the slight rise in the German series between 1985 and 1990.)

**Figure 4.2: 15-24 year old death rates in selected EU countries
(1970-95)**

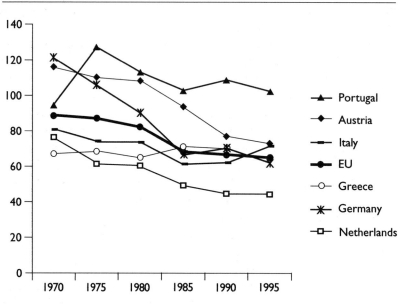

Note: The graph shows deaths per 100,000 in the age group.

Source: Table B2

There are obvious reasons why Europe has seen less improvement in bringing mortality rates down among older than younger children. Deaths among young children have been predominantly due to infectious disease, and in turn highly responsive to the improvements in nutrition, education and basic healthcare which have accompanied growing national wealth. In contrast, the majority of deaths among older groups are related to behaviour, making interventions harder to determine and to implement. Furthermore, these behavioural issues have themselves grown in size with economic development, which has brought with it the rise of motorised transport and, often, increased violence and the breakup of traditional social networks.

Unfortunately, therefore, premature mortality is still common enough in Europe to make it a useful measure of well-being, among both older and younger children. (If mortality among all three of the age groups shown in Table 4.1 were to converge on those of Sweden, there would be 25,000 fewer deaths in the EU among those aged under 25.) And in keeping with Sen's third argument, mortality indicators may also proxy other problems that may be difficult to measure by other means. The two death rates examined below are thus chosen for two reasons: as significant contributors to remaining child and youth mortality in Europe, and because they represent wider problems faced by the young in industrialised societies today.

First, we look at traffic death rates among the 5–14 age group, on the grounds that the rise in the use of the car has presented one of the greatest changes of recent decades to children's safety and independence. While many children benefit from the increased mobility rising car ownership has afforded their families, the same development has led to significant new constraints on their own personal freedom. Activities which their parents may have taken for granted – playing football in the street, cycling to school – are out of bounds to many European children today. Unfortunately, mortality rates are almost certainly not the best way to measure the effect the car has had on children's freedom of movement: although they may proxy the wider number of non-fatal accidents (which are difficult to compare across countries), accident rates will be affected by the degree to which parents adapt to the perceived threat (by keeping children indoors) as well as by the extent to which cars are kept in check by safety measures and pedestrian zones. This problem is discussed further below. Still, taken in conjunction with other data, the mortality rate gives us some insight into the problem – while also, of course, giving us direct information about the most tragic outcome of the proliferation of the car.

The second mortality measure we look at is the death rate of young men from suicide and self-inflicted injury, a problem of increasing concern in many industrialised countries. Suicide death rates among the young have been rising significantly in a number of countries in Europe, with men particularly affected. In addition to the waste of human potential each death represents, the level of youth suicide in a country suggests itself as one of the few available proxies for a wider phenomenon of stress, despair and disaffection affecting young people.

Child deaths from motor vehicle accidents

Motor vehicle accidents are now the single most important killer of children in Europe between the ages of 5 and 14. In 1994 they were responsible for 20% of deaths of both boys and girls of this age group – a total of 1,500 children killed on European roads. However, this still represents a considerable improvement on 30 years ago: in 1960 3,500 children in this age group were killed. So despite the increasing level of car ownership, Europe has seen a steady improvement in road safety:

between 1960 and 1994 the death rate for children aged 5-14 halved from 7.2 to 3.6 per 100,000. This apparent success raises two questions. First, how universal is the pattern: are all European children sharing in improvements? And second, what can we say about how far falling death rates are due to restrictions on children and how far to curbs on the speed and reach of traffic?

Figure 4.3 shows the main trends in road accident mortality rates for 5-14 year olds with data for selected countries. Most countries experienced a peak in the death rate in 1970, although the peak is at various different levels: Germany and Denmark (not shown), for instance, reach a maximum of 16 deaths per 100,000, compared to Austria and the Netherlands (12), and Italy and Ireland (9). From the early 1970s on, there is a steady decline in fatality rates such that by 1994 the death rate varies between 3 and 5 deaths per 100,000 in most of Europe.

The Southern European Cohesion countries provide an exception to this rule. In Portugal and Spain road death rates keep rising until 1980 and in Greece until 1990: in all three countries death rates in 1994 are higher than in 1960. The trend in Portugal is particularly striking: the number of children killed in road accidents per 100,000 doubled from 6 to 12 between 1960 and 1975, before falling back to 8 by 1994.

Naturally, this different trend in the Cohesion countries is explained by their later development: as the number of traffic accidents is to some extent a factor of the number of cars, surviving the threat of death by traffic accident is one welfare indicator likely to be negatively correlated with GDP. Greece and Spain in particular start off in 1960 with much lower traffic death rates than any of the more advanced European countries, and so the fact that these rates increase over the period is of little surprise.

However, there is clearly a point at which traffic accidents no longer increase with income, and countries turn their attention to improving road safety measures – hence the 1970 turnaround in Northern Europe. The Cohesion countries appear to have reached this turning point already: the road death rate in Portugal, as noted, has been falling since 1980; while in Greece the death rate fell in the first half of this decade, although it is too early to say whether this is a permanent trend. It is also worth noting that, even in Portugal, rates in the late 1970s did not reach the highest level of the 1970 peak: the pattern of road death rates in Portugal is an echo of the Austrian trend, for instance, rather than the German one.

The graph also includes measures of convergence from 1970 onwards. Both standard deviation and maximum/minimum ratio fell considerably between 1970 and 1985. Since then, however, the standard deviation has been stable while the maximum/minimum ratio has been on the rise. This is due, on the one hand, to continuing progress in reducing deaths in Sweden, and, on the other, to Portugal's failure to keep pace with the rest of Europe.

Figure 4.3: Deaths from motor vehicle accidents among children aged 5-14 in selected EU countries (1960-94)

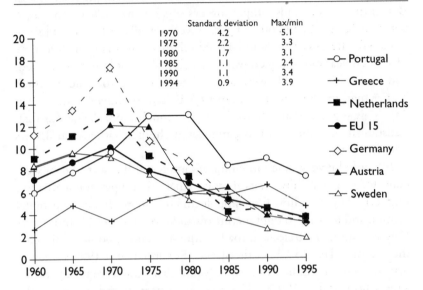

Note: The graph shows death per 100,000 in the age group. The standard deviation and the EU 15 rate are the weighted figures.

Source: Table B3

As suggested above, however, there is a potential problem with reaching conclusions about children's welfare on the basis of road death figures. It has been argued that road accidents are falling, not because of increased safety on the roads, but because parents are keeping their children cooped up at home away from traffic and other perceived dangers. A study for the UK Policy Studies Institute argues that "the streets have not become safer; they have become ... extremely dangerous. It is the response to this danger, by both children and their parents, that has contained the road accident death rate." (Hillman et al, 1990, p 2; see also Hillman, 1993). For instance, according to the study, in 1971 80% of British 7 and 8 year olds went to school on their own, but in 1990 only 9% were allowed to do so (Hillman et al, 1990, p 106)[5]. Half of 9 year olds in

1990 were allowed to cross the road unaccompanied, compared to 70% in 1971 (Hillman et al, 1990, p 44). Thus while European children may be less likely to be killed in traffic today than 20 years ago, this may be at the cost of a deteriorating quality of life for the young.

Once children's effective independence is considered alongside road fatality statistics, comparisons of road death rates across countries become complicated. For example, the Netherlands, Germany and the UK have near identical child death rates from traffic accidents in the early 1990s. But in the Netherlands sample surveys suggest that 61% of boys aged between 12 and 14 and 60% of girls travel most places by bike, while in Britain the figures are 13% and 4%. Similarly, in Germany in 1990, 60% of 7 and 8 year olds sampled were travelling to school unaccompanied, and 90% of 9 year olds were allowed to cross the road alone; much higher than the figures given above for Britain (Hillman et al, 1990, p 73). This suggests that UK roads may be much more dangerous than statistics suggest and that it is parents and children rather than drivers who have adapted.

It would be very much in children's interest if this sort of data were collected systematically. In its absence, what other types of information might shed light on how far falling death rates are really due to parental caution and how far to tighter controls and more responsible motorists? One way might be to look at road death rates among poorer children – those more likely to be on the street. For instance, a 1990 survey of primary school children in Lisbon found that 68% were unsupervised after school (Silva, 1997). This may be a partial explanation of the higher child death rate in Portugal. In Britain, a child from Social Class VI is more than four times as likely to be killed in a traffic accident as a child from Social Class I (Commission on Social Justice/IPPR, 1994, p 44), putting poorer children in Britain at similar or greater risk to the average child in Portugal. The problem with this approach, however, is that, while a disparity in fatality rates between social classes is good evidence that the roads are not as safe as the averages make them appear, the opposite is not necessarily true. An absence of such disparities may indicate that all children are supervised, rather than that even those on the streets are safe.

An alternative way of assessing the extent of children's diminishing independence may be to look at child road death rates within the context of trends in road deaths in the wider population. Is road safety improving in general, or are children simply being better protected from constant or increased dangers? Evidence suggests that in most of Europe roads are becoming safer for all, but that children have benefited more than other groups. As one illustration, Figure 4.4 shows road death rates in 1994 relative to those in 1970 for two groups of males: 5–14 year olds on the horizontal axis, and 15–24 year olds (the age range at which most young people become fully independent for the first time) on the vertical axis.

Figure 4.4: Road death rates in 1994 for two groups of young males, relative to those in 1970

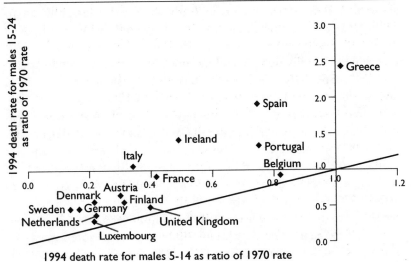

1994 death rate for males 5-14 as ratio of 1970 rate

Source: Table B4

All points in the graph are above the 45 degree line, meaning that child rates have fallen by more than rates for young people. In most countries child death rates are a third or less of what they were in 1970, while death rates for young people are still at least half of the 1970 level. In the Cohesion countries, child death rates have fallen (except in Greece) while rates for young men have actually risen over the period – the points are all well above the horizontal axis. A scatterplot of child death rates against those for the whole population shows a very similar picture. It does seem as though children are being increasingly insulated from traffic death rates in wider groups, in turn suggesting that it may be their behaviour more than that of the traffic which is being curbed.

Deaths of young men from suicide and self-inflicted injury

Traffic deaths are still the leading cause of death for young people in their late teens and early twenties. But it is the second most common cause of death for this age group, suicide and self-inflicted injury, which is attracting increasing concern. In part this is because suicide is responsible for a growing number of early deaths: while Figure 4.4 shows that in most of Europe road death rates for this age group are in decline, the average suicide rate for 15-24 year olds has grown by 40% since 1970. In part it is because a rising suicide rate suggests a wider phenomenon of disaffection and malaise among young people. Young men are particularly affected: over four times as many young men as young women die from suicide each year[6]. In 1994 over 3,000 males and some 750 females between the ages of 15 and 24 are recorded as having taken their own lives in the EU, and an additional 800 males and nearly 200 females died from violent causes undetermined whether deliberate or not[7]. Furthermore, in absolute numbers, suicides for men have gone up while those for women have remained fairly constant: in 1970 2,200 men and 800 women in this age group were recorded as having taken their lives, with 300 men and just over a hundred women recorded as having died through undetermined violence. (The population of both men and women aged 15-24 rose by some 5% over this period.)

The importance of including figures for deaths from undetermined causes arises from the problems involved in the classification of suicide deaths. It is widely held that official suicide statistics significantly underestimate the true number of suicides (see, for example, Pescosolido and Mendelsohn, 1986; Diekstra et al, 1995). A suicide death is one which is self-inflicted and intended, and the establishment of intent after death is not always easy. In many cases the decision hinges on witness testimony about the dead person's circumstances and state of mind, which introduces an element of uncertainty. In an investigation of verdicts reached on deaths of people run over by London Underground trains, Taylor (1982) illustrates how apparently identical deaths can end up being classified differently purely on the basis of whether or not a witness testifies that the person had seemed depressed.

This room for ambiguity is likely to result in a universal downward bias in suicide figures, as coroners and magistrates usually prefer to record an open verdict if in doubt, rather than cause unnecessary distress to surviving family. The key question for a cross-national comparison of suicide rates, however, is whether the degree of the bias is likely to vary across countries. There are two reasons to believe that it might. First, the taboo associated with suicide varies, providing differing motivations to disguise the circumstances of death. The long accepted inverse relationship Durkheim established between Catholicism and suicide rates is now often put down to a greater degree of under-reporting of suicide in Catholic countries (for example Pescosolido and Mendelsohn, 1986). Second, the procedures used to register cause of death themselves vary across countries. In particular, in England and Wales in order to record a death as a suicide a coroner must prove 'beyond reasonable doubt' that a person intended to take their own life – a relic of the times where a suicide verdict was a criminal verdict. No other European country has a comparable system: generally evidence of intent is not required and the decision on cause of death is made "on the balance of probabilities" (Madge, 1999).

In the case of England and Wales, it is now widely accepted that more realistic levels of suicide are achieved by combining suicide verdicts with deaths from undetermined causes (see Charlton et al, 1992; DoH, 1992). In this book we take this combined definition for all countries, both to ensure that (at least in one sense) we compare like with like, and because this should also have the effect of making suicide figures more representative for countries in which suicide is still relatively taboo. In fact, this approach turns out to increase noticeably only the rates in Portugal, which has a very low official suicide rate which is tripled by the inclusion of undetermined deaths, and, to a lesser extent, the UK, Sweden, Denmark and France. (In the other Catholic or Orthodox countries of Europe – Greece, Spain, Italy, Austria and Ireland – using this definition has little impact[8].) Even this definition has problems, of course: some undetermined deaths may be accidental, and some suicides may be recorded as fully accidental rather than as undetermined – for instance there are suggestions that youth deaths in car accidents are often disguised suicides (see, for example, Hassall, 1997, on the latter, and Madge and Harvey, 1999, on the general problem). But it is as close as we can get with publicly available data. As a word of final encouragement, Diekstra et al (1995) conclude their survey of studies of measurement error in suicide rates by noting that "these errors are more or less random, at least to an extent that allows useful comparisons to be made between countries, between socio-demographic groups, and over time" (p 695).

Measured in the broader way then, we find that male suicide rates are rising across the EU, although at several different speeds[9]. Figure 4.5

illustrates the main trends since 1970. The slow but steady increase in
the EU average reflects trends in the UK, Denmark, Belgium and France,
all of which have rates at roughly similar levels. A much better record is
found in parts of Southern Europe, the Italian trend representing similar
patterns in Spain and Greece: while suicides are also on the increase in
these countries they are still much below average. The Netherlands
(not shown) has a rate just above that of Italy.

Not all of Southern Europe does so well, however. The trend in
Portugal is very similar to that shown for Ireland. In both countries
suicides start very low but climb steadily, surpassing the EU average in
the mid-1980s. Ireland is also unique in displaying a steep increase in
suicides in the first half of the 1990s (Portugal records a considerable
drop between 1990 and 1994).

**Figure 4.5: Death rates from suicide and unexplained violence among
males aged 15-24 in selected EU countries (1970-94)**

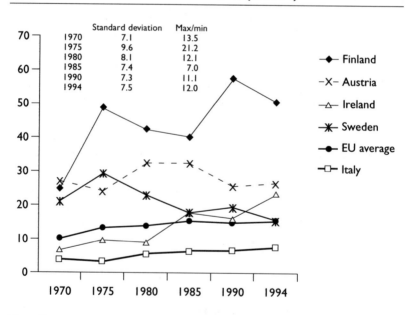

Note: The graph shows deaths per 100,000 in the age group.

Source: Table B5

But the really striking phenomenon illustrated in Figure 4.5 is the very
different patterns followed since 1970 by countries in Northern and
Central Europe. Austria, Finland, Sweden and Germany (which follows
roughly the Swedish trend) all started off in 1970 with fairly similar

suicide rates. Since then rates in Sweden and Germany have (alone in Europe) slowly fallen, the Austrian rate has remained fairly stable and suicides in Finland have increased dramatically.

What these differing patterns boil down to in terms of change in the overall degree of dispersion is shown by the figures for the standard deviation and the ratio of maximum to minimum. The maximum/ minimum ratio is largely driven by the pattern of Finnish suicide rates, rising to 1975, then falling to 1985 before rising again over the following decade. The ratio in 1994 is in fact lower than that in 1970, but this is due to a rise in the minimum (Greece). The standard deviation fell during the decade to 1985 but has remained constant since, while the fall itself has not been enough to compensate for the increase between 1970 and 1975. In sum, since 1985 there has been no convergence in youth suicide rates, while convergence in the previous decade could be classified as *negative* convergence given the background of the rising mean.

What explains these trends – both the general rise in youth suicide across Europe and the particularly dramatic pattern followed in Finland? High male mortality in Finland is a phenomenon which Finnish researchers have long been aware of, but for which satisfactory explanations are still lacking. In a paper appropriately entitled 'The mystery of the premature mortality of Finnish men', Valkonen (1985) writes:

> Violent and risk-taking behaviour seems to be characteristic of the male role in Finnish culture, especially among the working class and in Eastern Finland. This role often manifests itself in uncontrolled drinking. The roots of this (hypothetical) violent Finnish male role are perhaps to be found as early as the traditional rural culture, but the role may also have been influenced by the violence connected with the Civil War [1918] and the class situation after it. (Valkonen, 1985, p 240)

Yet while the nature of the Finnish soul may be a factor behind high suicide rates in Finland in general, it does not make sense of the fact that the suicide rate for young men has doubled since 1970, nor of the fact that it has done so while the rate in neighbouring Sweden has been falling. The same is true of other standard explanations of differing suicide rates, such as the availability of a means of death. Access to guns is relatively widespread in Finland as the hunting tradition is strong, and shooting deaths appear to be an unusually common means of suicide for young Finns (Madge, 1999), but again, this is a better explanation of a high level of suicide than of an increase over time. There is no evidence that increase in suicides by shooting in Finland has been accompanied by a change in the availability of firearms (Ohberg et al, 1996) – nor, for that matter, by a change in the availability of alcohol.

Some factor which has changed or intensified in Finland is required as an explanation. A link is often made between unemployment and psychological ill-health, particularly in men (see Morrell et al, 1998, for a good survey of the literature on the relation between unemployment and young people's health; Viren, 1996, for some evidence of an historical link between unemployment and suicide in Finland in particular). But has unemployment been much worse in Finland than elsewhere over this period, or likely to have had a deeper impact on young men? Ironically, the period at which Finland did suffer an unusually deep recession, the early 1990s (youth unemployment as a share of the cohort rose from 4% to nearly 20%, as shown in Chapter 3), is actually a time at which suicides were falling. Similarly, the big jump in the suicide rate in the late 1980s took place at a time when unemployment was stable or even falling: the cohort unemployment rate fell from 6% to 4% between 1983 and 1989. The pattern of youth suicide rates in Finland remains a mystery.

Concrete causes of the general European rise are also hard to pin down beyond vague formulations about social disintegration and alienation. Youth unemployment is again one explanation often put forward. Another, opposing, theory blames rising national incomes directly: some studies have suggested a positive relationship between national or community income and suicide (for example South, 1984; Huang, 1996), supporting this with the sociological explanation that suicide is less likely when people can attribute their misery to external events, such as their material circumstances (see, for example, Lester, 1992).

One key issue here of course is to put the rise in youth suicide in the context of suicide rates in general. Is the increase something which is specific to young people, or are youth suicide rates just one example of a wider social phenomenon? To do this we compared youth rates over the period with rates for an older age group, men between the ages of 45 and 54. It turns out that rises in youth suicide rates since the 1960s are largely matched by rises in the older age group: the phenomenon appears to be a general one, not just confined to the young. However, there are exceptions, which are illustrated in Figure 4.6. In Finland, while the peaks and troughs of the time-series have been the same for both age groups, the youth suicide rate has been gradually catching up with the rate for the older group. The same is true of the UK. In Austria, the youth suicide rate has remained stable while the rate for the 45-54s has fallen slightly. In Ireland the change over the full period is very similar for the two rates, but the rate for the older group has been much more volatile in the years between[10].

Figure 4.6: Male death rates from suicide for two age groups: 15-24s and 45-54s

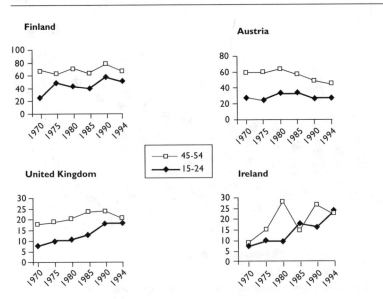

Note: The graph shows deaths per 100,000 in the age group.

Source: Tables B5 and B6

A final question of interest is the relation between suicides and homicides. Arguments have been put forward hypothesising both a positive relation (violent societies leading to more of both) and a negative relation (see Durkheim [1897] 1956)[11]. In fact, little relation can be found between the two mortality rates which cannot be explained by the experiences of one or two countries. Up until 1994, Finland is found to have a high homicide rate, driving a positive correlation if country figures are left unweighted. But in 1994 homicides in Finland are at roughly the average EU level, and the high homicide rate in Italy drives a *negative* correlation. With the exclusion of Italy – and Luxembourg – no relation emerges between the two rates, as can be seen in Figure 4.7. (Note the different scales: homicides among 15-24 year olds in Europe are far rarer events than suicides, at roughly one tenth the number. This contrasts sharply with the situation in the USA, where the homicide rate was some 70% higher than the suicide rate for young men of this age group in 1992 [WHO, 1996a][12].)

Figure 4.7: Suicide and homicide rates for young men aged 15-24, EU 15 (1994)

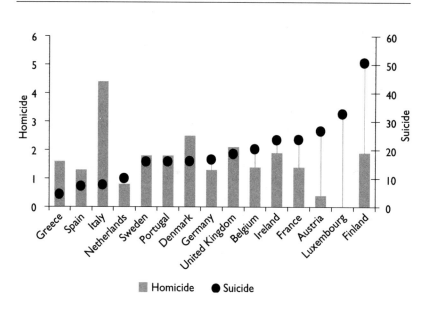

Notes: The graph shows deaths per 100,000 in the age group.

Source: Tables B5 and B7

The high homicide rate in Italy reflects the continuation of a steady increase in homicide deaths in that country since 1970, when Italy had one of the lower homicide rates in Europe. The other country which stands out in Figure 4.7 is Luxembourg, which recorded no homicides for this group in 1994. However, the population of Luxembourg is too small for this to be given much importance: just one death would have given Luxembourg a rate of 4 in 100,000 for the age group[13].

Conclusions: convergence in mortality?

To conclude, this chapter has illustrated the significant progress made in Europe in bringing down under-5 mortality rates, and through them death rates for all children. Rates of death for the under-20s have halved even since the early 1970s. With the less developed countries of Southern Europe (and Portugal in particular) exhibiting especially rapid progress, cross-country disparities in under-5 mortality and in total child mortality have been dramatically reduced.

Child death rates from traffic accidents have also converged considerably since 1960, although most progress was made prior to the mid-1980s. In the last decade disparities in road accident rates have tended to stagnate. In part this is due to Portugal, where death rates are falling too slowly to keep up with the rest of Europe; but in part to continuing achievements in countries where road deaths are already relatively rare.

However, we have also pointed out that it is difficult to know how far falling road fatality rates are due to additional restrictions being placed on the child rather than on the car. The fact that in most of Europe traffic death rates are coming down for all age groups, not just for children, is good news. But road death rate data really need to be supplemented by data on children's activities such as bicycle use and unaccompanied journeys to school if we are to have a more complete picture of what the rise in the use of the car has meant for children's independence. The small amount of this type of data that exists so far suggests that there would be an interesting cross-national story to be told.

Finally, the suicide rate shows little sign of convergence. Responsibility for this can partly be pinned on Finland, where young males have shown a frightening increase in tendency to suicide: the suicide rate for 15-24s has doubled since 1970. In 1970 suicide rates for this group were similar in Finland and Sweden; today Finnish young men are three times as likely to die from suicide as Swedish young men. However, while the problem appears of very serious proportions in Finland, the suicide rate is also a cause for concern across much of Europe. If Finland is excluded, we find that the standard deviation falls slowly between 1975 and 1995, but this has been convergence not to a low point but to a high to middling point. While Sweden, Austria and Germany have seen suicide rates stagnate or fall from relatively high levels, all other countries have seen rates rise. Besides Finland, the increase has been particularly sharp in Ireland, where youth suicide rates are now the third highest in Europe. Explaining these increases is beyond the scope of this book, but it is an area which demands further attention.

Notes

[1] *Relative* disparities also fell considerably over this period: the coefficient of variation fell by about two thirds between 1970 and 1990. Since 1990 it has risen slightly, but this is due to significant progress in reducing mortality by the two best-performing countries, Sweden (as shown in Figure 4.1) and Luxembourg (the unweighted measure rises more substantially – see Appendix Table B1). Persistent disparities in child and infant mortality across Europe seem to be partly explained by persistent differences in GDP: there is a negative correlation of −0.45 between IMR and per capita GDP in 1993. (See also the correlation with under-5 mortality in Table 2.1.) But this is driven entirely by the extremes – the performances of Luxembourg at the top and Greece and Portugal at the bottom. Remaining differences may owe something to the degree of disparity in child health *inside* certain countries, between social or regional groups. For instance, in Italy in 1991 infant mortality varied from 5.2 in the North West to 11.8 in the South (Saraceno, 1997, Table 10.1); while in England and Wales the rate varied from around 7 for Social Class I to 11 for Social Class VI, with the children of lone mothers recording a rate of around 14 (Commission on Social Justice/IPPR, 1994, Figure 1.11). In Sweden, in contrast, the rates for the top and bottom classes were similar at about 5, with the children born to lone mothers closer to 7 (Commission on Social Justice/IPPR, 1994, Figure 1.11).

[2] Under-5 mortality accounted for over 75% of deaths of under 20 year olds in 1970 and about 60% in 1995.

[3] The great bulk of deaths in Europe under the age of 5 are among infants (children aged under 1) – this is the case for over 80% of the 30,000 deaths among the under-5s in the EU 15 in 1995. And among infant deaths, about 45% are in the first week of life – and about 60% in the first month (Eurostat, 1997c, pp 178-9). As far as mortality among many young infants is concerned, the issue is not just one of reducing the number of deaths but also of preventing any disability stemming from the conditions generating that mortality, for example premature birth. This requires action to both reduce the factors leading to premature births (which include poverty, alcohol and drug abuse) and to improve intensive care for children who are prematurely born.

[4] The chances of dying before the age of 5 are still much higher than for either of these older age groups, however. It is not until a person reaches their late 30s/early 40s that the death rate again becomes as high as in the first years of life.

[5] Traffic danger was cited by 43% of parents as the primary reason for concern, compared to 21% who cited molestation and 21% who said their child was too unreliable.

[6] It is interesting, however, that 'parasuicide' (attempted suicide) seems to be more prevalent among young women than among young men: in the UK young women between 15 and 19 form the highest risk population group (The Samaritans, 1996). This may be because women happen to choose less violent means of death which allow room for discovery; or because female suicide attempts are more often cries for help than decisions to end life. Whichever is the explanation, parasuicide would in itself be an interesting measure of well-being, but data are obviously much less easily available.

[7] In comparison to both these categories, homicide was responsible for a tiny number of deaths. In 1994, for instance, there was less than one homicide for every 10 deaths from suicide or undetermined causes.

[8] It is worth noting that in Ireland a coroner is not permitted to pass a verdict of suicide: official recording of a death is determined at the statistical office on the basis of a confidential police report. This is likely to prevent sensitivity to family or community considerations from affecting the classification (Madge, 1999).

[9] If deaths from undetermined violence are excluded, suicide deaths are still found to be rising, but by slightly less: the EU average death rate for deaths classified as suicide and self-inflicted injury rose from 9.0 to 12.0 per 100,000 between 1970 and 1994; with undetermined violence included the rate rose from 10.4 to 14.9. The national trend is the same for the two measures in every country except Portugal, where the death rate for suicide alone falls over the period, while the rate for suicides and undetermined causes doubles.

[10] Figure 4.6 also allows us to see the differences in the *level* of suicide among younger and older age groups. In most European countries the suicide rate for 45-54 year old men is considerably higher than that for 15-24s (about double), as in the figure for Austria. Finland, Ireland and the UK are the exceptions: in 1994 in Finland the suicide rate for the older age group was only 20% higher than that for the younger; while in Ireland and the UK the rates were the same. In Finland and the UK this is because of the faster growth in youth rates; in Ireland, uniquely, youth rates have often been as high, although the rate for older men appears much more volatile.

[11] Durkheim expounds the thesis of an Italian school of criminology which argued that homicide and suicide are the same instinct manifesting itself in differently structured societies (Book Three, Chapter Two). Durkheim's own view is that there are different kinds of suicide. 'Egoistic' suicide is characterised by depression and apathy and is unlikely to coexist with homicide, "a violent act inseparable from passion" (see pp 356-7, English translation). 'Anomic' suicide, in contrast, springs from "a state of exasperation and irritated weariness which may turn against the person himself or another according to circumstances" (such as the moral constitution of the agent – 'a man of low morality will kill another rather than himself'). As anomic suicide is the 'more modern form', Durkheim implies that we should expect a positive relationship to dominate in the future.

[12] It is the homicide rate in the USA, of course, which stands out: the suicide rate is about 22 deaths per 100,000, similar to that in several European countries.

[13] Homicide rates have shown little convergence since 1970: the weighted coefficient of variation fell from 0.82 to 0.55 by 1980, but has since risen to 0.75. The mean has hovered at around 1.9 deaths per 100,000.

FIVE

Education

Education indicators can be divided into three types: input indicators, process indicators and output indicators. What interests us most about an education system is really its output, what people come out of school knowing, and how they are able to apply this knowledge. But output indicators which are consistent over time are notoriously difficult to find, and measures valid across countries with different examination systems are next to impossible to put together[1]. Most studies are therefore restricted to looking at input measures – the resources that go into education; and process indicators – enrolment rates and (where data are available) dropout rates and repetition rates.

In this chapter we look at trends in each of the first two types of indicator. We begin with public expenditure on education as a percentage of GNP, a standard input measure conducive to cross-national comparison and clearly reflecting government choice about priority given to education[2]. As a process indicator we choose the percentage of 16 year olds still in education; 16 is chosen as the first age at which education is no longer compulsory in the majority of EU countries[3]. Finally, we explore how far one new source of comparative data on output fits in with our findings by looking at some results from the Third International Mathematics and Science Study (TIMSS).

Expenditure as a percentage of GNP

Figure 5.1 shows the percentage of GNP spent on education since 1980 in a number of countries. The share of the young in the population varies across member states and we have standardised the data for each year to take account of the difference from the EU average in the share of 5-24 year olds (see Appendix Table C2 for details)[4]. In this way the adjusted figures allow a better comparison across countries (and time) of the proportion of national income devoted to public spending on education. This adjustment has a big impact on expenditure levels in Sweden and Ireland in particular: Sweden has a relatively low share of the population aged 5-24 (24% in 1995, for instance) and therefore adjusted expenditure figures are somewhat higher than unadjusted, while in Ireland this group makes up a relatively large share of the population (35% in 1995), and the adjusted expenditure figures are lower than the unadjusted. Commitment to public education in Sweden, in terms of spending, is higher than the raw data imply, while that in Ireland is lower. A smaller impact is seen on spending levels for Denmark, Finland and Germany (adjusted figures are higher) and for Portugal (adjusted figures are lower).

As Figure 5.1 shows, education expenditure seems to be broadly converging on the level of 5% of GNP. Spending in Sweden and the Netherlands falls from very high levels; in Spain, Greece and Portugal (not illustrated in the diagram) on the other hand, spending rises from very low levels, although the Cohesion Four nevertheless occupy the last four places in the ranking by the end of the period. (The trend in Ireland is an exception in this group.) Elsewhere, expenditure is stable at around 5% or 6% of GNP[5].

Figure 5.1: Public expenditure on education as a percentage of GNP, selected EU countries (1980-95)

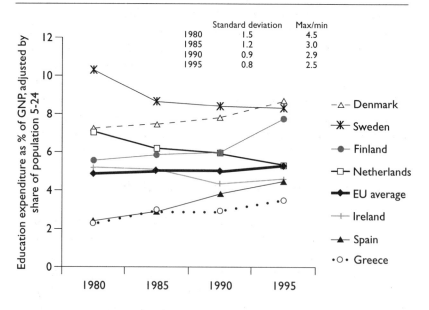

Note: The data are adjusted for the share of 5-24 year olds in each country.

Source: Table C2

The measures of dispersion given in the graph support the visual impression, showing reasonable evidence of convergence during the period – although mostly this took place during the 1980s. The smaller change of the early 1990s is due to rising expenditure in higher spending countries – Denmark and Finland – preventing Spain, Greece and Portugal from catching up despite their own progress[6].

The other interesting phenomenon is the contribution towards convergence made by countries where the education share has been *falling*, notably the Netherlands and Sweden. The Netherlands falls from the third highest spender on education, with a similar share to Denmark, down to the EU average. (GDP growth has been similar in Denmark and the Netherlands.) The UK and Ireland are the only other countries where the spending share falls much over the period, in the UK from 5.7% in 1980 to 5% in 1985 and subsequently, and in Ireland from 5.2% to 4.6%, but against a background of rapid GDP growth.

Finally, Figure 5.2 shows the division of expenditure by level of education for one point in time, to give an idea of whether cross-country disparities are concentrated at particular levels[7]. (We have again adjusted the data for differences in the age structure of the population.) The figure suggests that higher spending levels in Scandinavia can be explained in part by higher spending on secondary education, but are mostly attributable to expenditure at the tertiary level. Disparities may therefore be somewhat exaggerated: for example the Swedish tertiary education figure appears to be unique in including research expenditure. But higher levels of tertiary spending in Scandinavia are probably also due to spending on student grants and loans: Sweden and Denmark both spend over 15% of total education expenditure on financial aid for pupils/students, compared to an EU average of under 6%.

At the other end of the spectrum, Luxembourg emerges as a low spender but only because of the low level of expenditure on tertiary education (Luxembourg has no university and most young people study in neighbouring countries).

Figure 5.2: Public expenditure on education by level (1995)

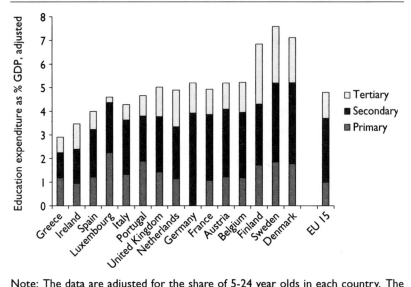

Note: The data are adjusted for the share of 5-24 year olds in each country. The German data do not distinguish primary and secondary levels separately.

Source: Table C3

Enrolment at age 16

Our process indicator, the share of 16 year olds in education, shows strong evidence of convergence over the period for which data are available[8]. This is illustrated in Figure 5.3 (data are missing for Denmark, Germany and Italy)[9]. Convergence is driven by strong achievement among countries which had been lagging behind, alongside understandably slower progress among countries which already had high shares of the population in education, notably Scandinavia. Not all the countries lagging behind are those which might be expected, however. The group includes Portugal and Spain, where less than 20% of 16 year olds were in education in the 1960s, but respectively 80% and 90% by 1994[10]. But it also includes the UK, where the share in education was just 27% at the start of the 1960s, less than that in Greece, Italy and Ireland, and still only 57% in 1990. By 1994, 82% of UK 16 year olds were in education. This improvement drove a sharp fall in the standard deviation between 1990 and 1994, although the UK position was still the fourth worst of the 14 countries for which data are available, and only just ahead of Greece, Portugal and Luxembourg[11].

Luxembourg presents an interesting case: in the mid–1960s it was the country with the best enrolment rate in Europe, and today it ranks bottom. As Figure 5.3 illustrates, this deterioration in its relative standing is not due to stagnation, but rather to a big drop in enrolment in the late 1960s. The explanation for this strange development is not clear, although it is worth noting that Austria experiences a similar phenomenon: enrolment drops from 71% in 1964/65 to 33% in 1970/74, recovering over the next two decades to reach 90% in the mid-1990s. It may simply be that there is a problem with the 1964/65 data for both countries. Even were this the case, however, Luxembourg would still stand out for its low enrolment rate in the 1990s – striking given that Luxembourg's GDP per capita is the highest in the EU. This surprising finding is supported by data from the 1995 Eurostat Labour Force Survey, which found that only 51% of 25-29 year olds in Luxembourg had completed upper secondary education. This is the same share as that found in Spain and Italy, and the second lowest in Europe after Portugal (36%); the EU average was 69% (Eurostat, 1997a, p 15).

What is driving rising enrolment? In part the trend must be explained by increases in the minimum school leaving age. But it is also likely to be related to both rising national income (education is a consumption as well as an investment good) and to changes in unemployment: lack of job opportunities for school leavers will encourage the young to stay on for post-compulsory education. Hence the rising levels of youth

Figure 5.3: Percentage of 16 year olds in education in selected EU countries (1965-95)

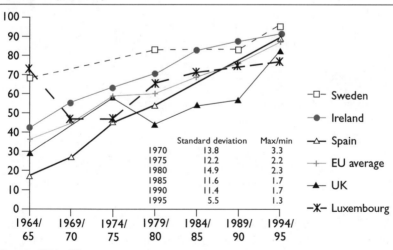

Source: Table C4

unemployment discussed in Chapter 3 are probably responsible in part for the trends in enrolment illustrated here[12].

Finally, Figure 5.4 shows the most recent figures for the two indicators together. Clearly we would expect a positive link between expenditure and enrolment: higher enrolment demands higher spending; while higher spending is an indication of a commitment to education which we would expect to affect (among other things) post-compulsory enrolment rates. Indeed, the top six countries ranked on spending as a share of GNP all have 16 year old enrolment over 90%, with enrolment on average lower among the lower spenders. The noticeable exceptions are Germany, Spain and Ireland, where enrolment appears high in relation to spending. In part, the peaks and troughs in the enrolment data simply reflect the law: in Germany and Belgium the school leaving age is 18, while in Portugal and Greece (among other countries) it is still 15.

Figure 5.4: Enrolment among 16 year olds and public spending on education (1994/95)

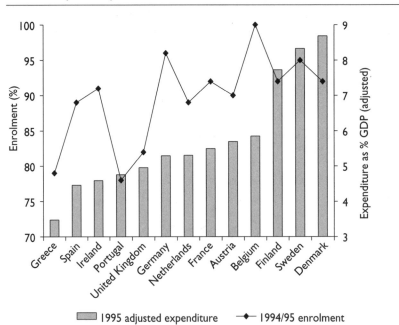

1995 adjusted expenditure   1994/95 enrolment

Note: The expenditure data are adjusted for the share of 5-24 year olds in each country.

Source: Tables C2 and C4

Output measures: the Third International Mathematics and Science Study

Principal interest lies in what children are learning, rather than simply how long schools are holding on to them. Unfortunately, no good time-series data exist on learning achievement for a sufficient number of countries, but the Third International Mathematics and Science Study (TIMSS) shows how pupils across Europe compared in achievement in maths and science in one recent year, 1994/95, and hence gives an idea of how far enrolment rate data might be misleading if we were to rely on them as the main indicator of educational progress (Beaton et al, 1996a, 1996b).

Figure 5.5 shows the percentage of 16 year olds in education against the percentage of eighth graders with TIMSS scores for science at or above the fiftieth percentile measured across all participating countries[13]. The average age of the children in these TIMSS data was 14 years old, which is below the minimum school leaving age in all the EU countries in the study; the variation in scores across the member states does not therefore reflect a different mix of children beyond compulsory school age from country to country.

The graph shows only a very weak correlation between staying-on rates and TIMSS success. Countries performing relatively badly in the TIMSS include low participation countries like Portugal and Greece, but also Denmark and France, where 16 year old enrolment is above 90%. Belgium is another country where less than half of pupils were found to be above the international median, despite the fact that all 16 year olds are in full-time education. (This, however, is entirely due to performance in French-speaking Belgium: 64% of children in Flemish-speaking schools were above the international median, compared to only 29% of children in French schools.) At the other end, the UK (a weighted average of results for England and Scotland) achieves the third best TIMSS result despite having the third worst enrolment record, while the Netherlands and Austria perform the best although ranking only around average on enrolment.

This weak relation illustrates the danger of reading enrolment rates as if they were measures of educational quality. Indeed, measures of educational standards are themselves not without contradictions. The TIMSS scores given in Figure 5.5 are for science results for eighth graders, but results are also available for seventh graders and for mathematics achievement. While there is a very high correlation within each subject area for scores for seventh and eighth graders (0.96 for

Figure 5.5: Relationship between TIMSS Science results for 14 year olds and 16 year old enrolment rates in 1994/95

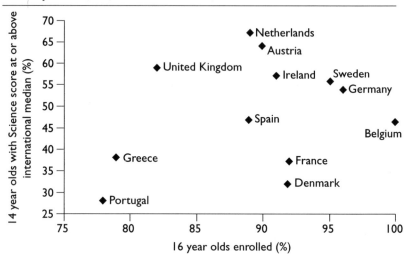

Notes: The score for the UK is a weighted average of scores for England and Scotland. The score for Belgium is a straight average of scores for the Flemish and French educational systems.

Source: Table C6

maths, 0.97 for science), there is less correlation between achievements in the two areas (0.68 for seventh graders, 0.55 for eighth graders). The rankings of France, Belgium and Denmark benefit particularly from a measure which takes mathematics achievement: France and Belgium rank in the top four with the Netherlands and Austria on maths, while in Denmark 47% of pupils were above the international median in maths compared to only 32% in science. The UK, in contrast, slips in the rankings when judged on maths rather than on science: 48% of English pupils were above the median in maths compared to 60% in science[14].

Results from an alternative measure of learning achievement, the OECD *International Adult Literacy Survey* (OECD, 1997a), give a different impression again for an older age group, 16-25 year olds. Like the TIMSS, the data relate to the early 1990s, but cover just six EU member states. Sweden, the Netherlands, Germany and Flemish-speaking Belgium all score well under the survey as under the TIMSS (no data were collected in French speaking Belgium). But the UK and Ireland both come out badly. For instance, over 75% of pupils in Sweden, Flemish-speaking Belgium and the Netherlands and 66% of pupils in Germany were classified at or above the third of five levels of 'document literacy', compared to only 56% of this age group in the UK, and to 50% in Ireland. Not only then are enrolment data far from adequate as a measure of educational well-being, but it is clear that measures of educational standards themselves must be handled with care.

Notes

[1] Recent suggestions by UK employers and universities that there has been a 'devaluation' of the 'gold standard' of the A level (the final school exams in England and Wales) provide evidence that even within a single country it is difficult to know whether exam results can be compared across years. Seventeen per cent of pupils received the top grade in 1998, compared to 11% 10 years previously (see, for example, *The Guardian*, 20 August 1998). In the USA, declining average performance in a standardised aptitude test of high school students since the 1960s has provoked much discussion of the causes, including the possibility that increases in enrolment have led to a change in the composition of the pool of students taking the test, rendering information on changes in mean scores of little value (Murray, 1996).

[2] The 1997 OECD report on education indicators, *Education at a glance*, notes that "the share of total financial resources devoted to education is one of the key choices made in each country" (OECD, 1997b, p 51). In fact, as the report goes on to point out, public expenditure is now only one part of this choice, with resources coming from private sources of funding playing an increasingly important role. But private resources are still responsible for a very small share of the total in most EU countries (see OECD, 1997b, p 52), while time-series data which include private funding are not easily available. There is also independent reason to focus on the share spent publicly if our interest is in the priority given to education by government.

[3] The minimum school-leaving age in 1994/95 was 15 in all EU countries except Italy (14), the UK, France and the Netherlands (16) and Belgium and Germany (18) (UNESCO, 1998a). The school-leaving age in Italy has been increased to 15 as of the academic year 1998-99.

[4] We follow one of the methods used by the OECD in *Education at a glance* (OECD, 1997b) although we use a slightly different population share (and the OECD adjustment is in relation to the OECD rather than the EU average).

[5] Five per cent of GNP should not be viewed as a 'natural' figure, but neither is there reason to expect the share of spending on education in national

income to rise indefinitely, especially in industrialised countries with high enrolment rates at all levels of education.

[6] Some care needs to be taken in interpreting these big rises in education shares, as what they mean for real expenditure levels will clearly depend on what is happening to national income. For instance, Finland suffered a severe recession in the 1990s: GDP fell by over 10% between 1990 and 1993, recovering only by 1996 (Eurostat, 1997d, p 208). The large increase in the Finnish education share in the 1990s thus reflects the protection of education spending in time of recession. In Denmark, in contrast, the education share rose against a background of steady GDP growth.

[7] The following two paragraphs and Figure 5.2 are based on Eurostat (1998a). Unfortunately total spending levels given differ somewhat from the UNESCO figures presented in Figure 5.1. In part this is because the Eurostat figures are for education expenditure as a share of GDP, while those from UNESCO are as a share of GNP (this may affect data for Ireland in particular, for reasons given in Chapter 3). But differing definitions of education expenditure and discrepancies in the calculations of GDP are also likely to be responsible. These are a common problem in comparing public expenditure figures from different sources. For example, Puryear (1995) finds that "OECD figures indicated that the proportion of total public expenditure going to education in Austria in 1988 was nearly half as great as did UNESCO's figures".

[8] 'In education' means in full-time education, including technical and vocational education.

[9] There are too many missing observations to put together a series for Denmark, Germany or Italy. For six of the remaining 12 countries, data were interpolated for certain years on the basis of those for preceding and following years. These points can be identified in Figure 5.3 as no data marker is given.

[10] The minimum school-leaving age has increased over the period from 11 to 15 in Portugal and from 12 to 15 in Spain.

[11] The UNESCO administrative enrolment data used here was compared to responses to the question 'How old were you when you left full-time education?', in the Eurobarometer surveys used in Chapter 7. The two series are reassuringly similar. For instance, there is a correlation of 0.91 between national 16 year old enrolment rates in 1989/90 and the share of 16-24 year olds interviewed between 1990 and 1994 who claimed not to have left school

at age 16 or below. Seventy-eight per cent of Spaniards put themselves into this category (UNESCO enrolment rate 77%), 82% of Irish (87%), 60% of Portuguese (68%) and 55% of those in the UK (57%). These data are given in Appendix Table C5.

[12] Evidence for the UK, for example, shows changes in enrolment at the post-compulsory level to be indeed related to income and unemployment (Pissarides, 1981; Whitfield and Wilson, 1991).

[13] We could have looked at average scores rather than the share of pupils above the international median, but the latter is more appealing in principle since it takes account of the spread at the bottom of the distribution of scores for each country, as well as the overall position of the distribution as summarised by the average. In fact there is near complete correlation between the two (0.99) on all measures mentioned in this chapter.

[14] Prais (1997) considers the maths results for pupils in England in detail, comparing them with other European countries in the TIMSS. He also makes comparisons of England's relative position with that shown in earlier international studies of maths achievement (which contained fewer countries) conducted, like the TIMSS, by the International Association for the Evaluation of Educational Achievement. His conclusion was that the TIMSS repeated the broad result of the earlier studies of about a year's lag in achievement in England compared to other Western European countries.

SIX

Teenage fertility

It is widely accepted that teenage fertility is associated with negative outcomes for both mother and child. A series of studies in the UK and the US suggest that women who give birth before they are 20 are less likely than other women to finish school, more likely to be poor at the end of their 20s, and more likely to bring up their children as single mothers (Hofferth and Moore, 1979; Furstenburg et al, 1987; Maynard, 1997; Social Exclusion Unit, 1999). The disadvantages for their children appear to begin at birth and last into adolescence. Children of teenage mothers seem to be more likely to be born with low birth weight, less likely to be breastfed and fully immunised, and more likely to die in the first year of life. They have also been shown to be at greater risk of physical abuse and accidental injury, and to do less well in education (for the UK see Butler et al, 1981; Manlove, 1997; and Social Exclusion Unit, 1999; for the US see Furstenburg et al, 1987; and Maynard, 1997).

Despite the general perception, however, the causal impact of teenage fertility on subsequent events in the life of mother and child in industrialised countries is in fact the subject of genuine debate. The evidence of the harmful nature of teenage births is not as conclusive as it seems at first sight. We therefore start this chapter by considering in more detail the extent to which teenage fertility really can be considered an (inverse) measure of young women's well-being, illustrating the arguments with evidence from the EU country where, as we will see later, teenage fertility is at its highest, the UK[1].

What information is conveyed by teenage fertility?

Not all studies in industrialised countries have found a link between a mother's age at birth and the outcomes for her child, either in terms of immediate birth outcomes or in a longer developmental perspective. Examples of studies where no link is found are those by Osbourne et al (1981) on obstetric outcomes of women in Glasgow, and Wolkind and Kruk (1985) on child health, development and behaviour of children in the seven years after birth. Macintyre and Cunningham-Burley (1993) give a list of further references: they argue that these studies have less impact on public perception than those which find evidence of a negative link:"Because of the perception that teenage pregnancy is a problem ... investigators or their readers may focus on the evidence of difficulties and ignore evidence of lack of them" (p 65).

That women who become mothers as teenagers are themselves less likely than their peers to do well in education and in the labour market seems to be less controversial. However, here the nature of the relation has come under question: it is not clear that teenage childbearing is itself the cause of the outcomes observed, rather than merely an associated factor. Teenage motherhood is very strongly correlated with a background of social and economic disadvantage, and it may be this disadvantage itself which is responsible for the mother's life path[2]. (It may also, of course, drive health and development outcomes of the child.) While most studies do control for a series of socio-economic factors, they have been open to the criticism that important background variables are likely to remain unobserved. Studies from the US which try to avoid this problem by using carefully selected control groups reach much less clear cut conclusions[3].

Nevertheless, even if the causal impact of teenage birth on future outcomes for mother and child is uncertain, there does seem to be good reason to use it as a negative indicator in itself of the current well-being of teenage girls. There is strong evidence in the UK that most teenage pregnancies do not represent genuine choices on the part of young women[4]. Rather, they reflect, on the one hand, a lack of the information, the access to contraception, and/or the confidence which would allow them to prevent unwanted pregnancies; and on the other, the absence of educational and job opportunities which would motivate them to avoid early motherhood.

Surveys based on interviews with teenage mothers repeatedly suggest that the mothers were either badly informed about the need for contraception or were blocked from getting it by not knowing where to go, by embarrassment, or – if under 16 – by their parents[5]. (Sharpe, 1987; Allen, 1991; Phoenix, 1991; and Schofield, 1994 all paint a vivid picture of the problem.) None of these situations could be easily labelled as desirable. Teenage pregnancies can be seen as a measurable outcome of these problems.

It is not difficult to reconcile this view of teenage pregnancy with the evidence on the disadvantaged backgrounds of most teenage mothers. Access to contraception and abortion may be lower for this group, due to lack of information and more limited ability to travel to family planning clinics, for example. But in addition, girls from disadvantaged backgrounds have fewer alternative options available to them. Women with better educational records and fulfilling careers to look forward to clearly have much stronger reasons to avoid pregnancy than do women who are unemployed or in low-paid and repetitive jobs. This is not inconsistent with the view that the majority of teen pregnancies are accidents: clearly the incentive to be careful differs for different women. If they do become pregnant, more privileged women are much more likely to choose abortion[6]. All evidence suggests that teenagers with real alternatives do not choose early motherhood.

The teen fertility rate thus seems to be an important indicator of lack of information and lack of opportunities among young women in the UK. There are reasons, however, why this may not necessarily hold across the rest of Europe[7]. It is possible that in other parts of Europe teenage fertility has different connotations: there may be traditions of settling down earlier, with teenage births more likely to be planned. In fact, demographic trends across Europe are similar enough for this to be of little likely significance, but it is an issue explored in greater detail below in discussion of the share of teen births that take place within marriage, and also the share which take place to younger teenagers (16 year olds).

Trends in teenage birth rates

Figure 6.1 illustrates the main national trends in teenage fertility since 1960[8]. The broad European pattern is a peak in the teen birth rate in 1970, followed by steady decline since then, although, as the graph shows, there have been several exceptions. Denmark, which had a teenage birth rate over twice the EU average at the start of the period, peaks in the mid-1960s and then experiences rapid progress over the next two decades, passing below the EU average by 1980. At the same time, Greece rises equally quickly from one of the lowest rates in the EU to one of the highest. The path followed by Greece reflects similar, although less dramatic, trends in Spain, Ireland, Portugal and Italy: these countries start with fairly low birth rates in 1960 and then rise to a late peak in 1980 (Italy in 1975). Falling birth rates across northern Europe and this rise in the South are reflected in convergence in both dispersion measures between 1970 and 1975.

Figure 6.1: Age 15-19 birth rates, selected EU countries (1960-95)

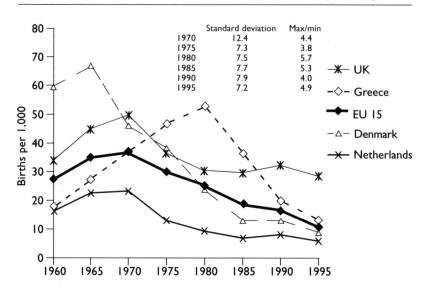

Note: Birth rates are calculated as all births to teenagers per 1,000 women aged 15-19 (see notes to Table D1 for more details).

Source: Table D1

From 1975 to 1990, however, the standard deviation is on the rise, while the maximum/minimum ratio rises, falls and then rises. The initial rise in both measures is due to 'overshooting' on the part of Greece and Portugal. Then, at the point at which rates in these countries start to come down, a new outlier emerges – the UK. Unlike the pattern in all other European countries, the birth rate in the UK has shown no tendency to decline since 1975, but has hovered around the rate of 30 births per 1,000 teenage women, compared to an overall EU figure of about 11 births by 1995 (and only 6 in the Netherlands). Because of the UK's relative size, this affects the weighted standard deviation. Since 1990, both the UK fertility rate and the standard deviation have fallen, but the latter in 1995 was still no lower than in 1975. Thus absolute disparities in the fertility rate were similar in 1975 and 1995. *Relative* disparities have actually gone up over the period, as measured by both the max/min ratio and the coefficient of variation, which has been rising steadily over the last 20 years.

How far do these trends simply reflect trends in overall fertility? The UK, for instance, has not experienced as rapid a decline in fertility rates as a number of other European countries. Does this go any way towards explaining the stability of teenage birth rates in the UK over the last 20 years? In fact, while the declining total fertility rate may explain some part of the general downward trend in teenage birth rates, it does not appear to be responsible for individual country trends. Birth rates for women aged 15-49 have been falling steadily in all countries, and at relatively similar speeds when compared to the varied pattern of teenage birth rates. The result is that teenage births as a percentage of the total actually look very similar to teenage birth rates themselves: a graph showing teen births as a percentage of the total would closely resemble Figure 6.1. (Data for births to 15-19 year olds as a share of total births are given in the Appendix in Table D2.)

There are then clearly factors which affect teenage fertility more than or differently than total fertility. On reflection this is not surprising: we might expect teenagers to have been more strongly affected than the general population by changes in the availability of contraception and abortion. In much of Europe, contraception became free and widely available sometime during the 1970s[9]. Abortion laws in most of non-Catholic Europe were reformed at about the same time to allow fairly unrestricted access to abortion in the first trimester[10].

Conception rates

While it is easy to specify increasing access to both contraception and abortion as an explanation of falling teenage fertility since the 1970s, the degree to which the decline is explained by one factor rather than the other is an important question. As explained earlier, our interest is in teenage births as an indicator of current well-being rather than as a determinant of later outcomes. As a measure of lack of opportunities for young women the teen birth rate itself seems the appropriate indicator, but as a measure of poor information and access to birth control our interest is really in conception rather than birth. The birth rate is frequently used as a rough proxy for the conception rate given that data on abortions are often not available or reliable[11]. However, it is certain to be the case that conception rates differ from birth rates considerably, both across countries and over time.

There are insufficient data on abortion throughout the period to enable us to establish the role played by the legalisation of abortion in bringing down the teen birth rate. There is some evidence that the share of teen pregnancies ending in abortion increased during the 1970s, and that this explains part but not all of the downward trend in teen births – conceptions appear to have decreased as well (for example on

Denmark see Rodman and Trost, 1986, p 63; and on the UK, Phoenix, 1991, p 40).

However, we do have evidence that the importance of abortion varies considerably even across countries in which it is freely available. Figure 6.2 shows births and abortions in 1990 for the 10 countries for which data are available (others tend to be those in which abortion is still illegal and no statistics are kept).

Figure 6.2: Birth and abortion rates for 15-19 year olds (1990)

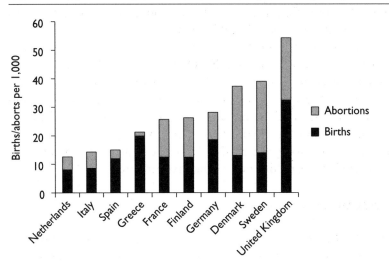

Sources: Tables D1 and D3

When abortions and births are added together in this way to form a rough teenage conception rate, there is some re-ranking of countries. In particular, the Scandinavian countries, and especially Denmark and Sweden, rank much less well on conception rates than on birth rates: more than half of teen pregnancies in both countries end in abortion, and it is high levels of abortions rather than contraception which is keeping birth rates down. In contrast, the Netherlands has one of the lowest abortion rates as well as the lowest birth rate in Europe – and this despite having one of the most liberal abortion laws in the world. (The Netherlands, along with Spain and England and Wales, is also one of the places non-resident women travel to obtain abortions, so this will swell the figures somewhat[12].) The UK remains the country with the worst record when ranked on conceptions, despite an abortion rate which is lower than those in Scandinavia.

Births to unmarried teenagers and to younger teens

Finally, we can get a little more insight into cross-country differences in teenage birth rates by breaking them down into more detail in two ways – by marital status and by age. As with abortions, this cannot be done for every year with the data we have, but even a static picture in one year can help us shed light on how far a teen birth in one country is a similar phenomenon to one in another. Births to unmarried and to younger teenagers are less likely to have been wanted: the possibility that these are simply young women choosing to settle down early is smaller.

Unfortunately, of course, grouping teen mothers as married or unmarried does not pick up exactly the distinction we would like here. First, we only know whether women were married at the time of the birth; hence women who marry their partners *because* they are pregnant are indistinguishable from those who had decided to marry beforehand. Second, and perhaps more important, the growing incidence of cohabitation, particularly in Scandinavia, means that the unmarried group will include mothers in stable relationships which are effectively marriages along with mothers who are genuinely single. However, looked at with an eye on the role of cohabitation in each society, the breakdown ought to be of some interest.

Figure 6.3: Teen birth rate and percentage of teens giving birth who are unmarried (1995)

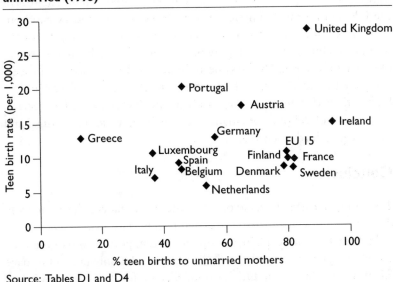

Source: Tables D1 and D4

The share of teenage births to unmarried mothers varies widely across countries, from a low of 11% in Greece to a high of 93% in Ireland – see Figure 6.3. In Italy, Spain and Portugal the percentage is relatively low, at just over 40% of teen births, and here (and in Greece) this may reflect social mores which make it more likely that a pregnant teenager will face pressure to marry. The high share of extra-marital births in Sweden, Denmark and Finland will at least in part be explained by the high rate of cohabitation. However, in Ireland cohabitation is much less widespread and less likely to explain the high level of extra-marital teen births: these are more plausibly accidental pregnancies (20% of births to women of all ages in Ireland were extra-marital in 1994, compared to 50% in Sweden and 45% in Denmark). The same is true to a lesser extent of the UK, where one third of all babies are born outside marriage, while 85% of babies born to teenage mothers are extra-marital births.

The second way in which the teen birth rate can be broken down into more detail is by looking at the extent to which it is composed of births to younger rather than older teens. Several of the possible reasons for concern about teen births apply with more force the younger is the mother. As might be expected, the share of all teen births which are to younger teens tends to be higher in countries where teen birth rates are higher. Countries with low teen birth rates, in contrast, have the majority of teen births to 19 year olds. Thus, for instance, in the Netherlands over half of teen births are to 19 year olds, compared to less than 40% in the UK and Portugal. The result is that these two countries stand out even more with respect to the 16 year old birth rate than they do for the overall teen birth rate – see Figure 6.4. Indeed, the birth rate for 16 year olds in the UK is roughly the same as the average EU rate for *all* teenagers between 15 and 19; while the birth rate to Portuguese 16 year olds is higher than that to 15-19 year olds in the Netherlands, Italy, Spain, Denmark and Belgium. As many as 1% of 16 year olds in Portugal and the UK give birth each year[13].

Conclusions

Two things in particular stand out from the above analysis: the particularly dramatic improvement to the teenage fertility rate made in Denmark (which we have not explained), and the current poor record of the UK, with the highest teen birth rate in Europe and the only rate not to have fallen since 1980. If the UK is excluded, teen fertility rates show clear

Figure 6.4 : Birth rate for 16 year olds and for all 15-19 year olds (1994)

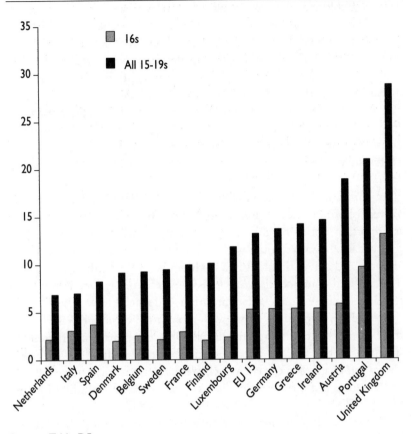

Source: Table D5

evidence of convergence across Europe since 1980. When the figures are broken down, we also find that a higher share of teen births in the UK are to younger teens than anywhere else in Europe, while only Ireland has a higher share of teen births to unmarried mothers.

These breakdowns suggest that the phenomenon of teenage fertility is more serious in the UK as well as being more widespread. Yet contraception is free in the UK and accessible through family planning clinics where anonymity is assured. On the surface, the system looks as liberal as that in the Netherlands, the country with the lowest teen birth rate (and, it seems, the lowest teen conception rate) in Europe.

The Dutch success in combating teenage pregnancy is generally put down to an open and unembarrassed attitude towards sex which allows sexual issues to be discussed frankly and clinics to be advertised widely.

This, for instance, was the conclusion of a conference held in the UK in 1994 to explore exactly this question ('Can we learn from the Dutch?' – see Forum for Family Planning, 1994, cited in Jacobson et al, 1995). Jacobson et al describe the Dutch system as one in which "[t]he teenager and the doctor feel comfortable discussing sexuality in a warm, mutually supporting atmosphere, requests for contraceptive services are not associated with shame or embarrassment [and] the media is willing to carry messages designed for young people about contraceptive services" (p 235)[14]. The result appears to be an atmosphere in which the use of contraception is "as ingrained as not going through a red light", as one Dutch survey respondent put it in the early 1980s (Jones et al, 1986, p 154).

In contrast, the situation in the UK may be better summed up by the 18 year old single mother in the late 1980s who said she had considered it important not to become pregnant, but: "I just stopped taking [the pill] because I wasn't going with anyone at the time then I just forgot about it and threw them away and that was it" (Phoenix, 1991, p 75). The fact that contraceptives are accessible in theory will be irrelevant if teenagers underestimate their importance, do not know where to get hold of them in practice or are too embarrassed to raise the issue with their partners. Legislation during the 1980s may have exacerbated the situation in the UK by a combination of cuts in funding to health clinics and changes in the law which seem to have made it more difficult for doctors and teachers to discuss sexual matters with underage teenagers[15].

As suggested in the introduction to this chapter, however, a second important factor in determining teenage births is likely to be the alternative opportunities young women face – or the lack of them. As noted there, teenage mothers in the UK come predominantly from disadvantaged backgrounds. While the fact that most teen pregnancies are unwanted belies the idea that teenagers actively choose motherhood as a more attractive alternative to unemployment or a dead-end job, women with few prospects clearly have less incentive to be careful about contraception, and also appear less likely to choose abortion. It may be difficult to use the teen birth rate as a cross-national indicator of lack of opportunity, as it is possible that circumstances in the UK make motherhood appear a more attractive escape route than elsewhere: in particular, the chance of receiving separate housing may mean teenagers in the UK associate motherhood with an independence not available to young women in Southern Europe. But it is likely that high teen births since the 1980s in the UK are in part explained by unemployment and social exclusion among the young.

The UK government's own recent analysis of teenage pregnancy, published as we finalised this book, is broadly in line with our conclusions, emphasising in particular the impact of low expectations and of ignorance – both of contraception and of what it is like to be a parent (Social Exclusion Unit, 1999)[16]. Part of the strategy proposed to ensure that the UK teen pregnancy rate converges towards the European average is a more open public discussion and awareness of the issue.

Notes

[1] We should emphasise that our discussion in this chapter does not have any clear relevance to teenage fertility in developing countries, where the social, cultural and economic factors surrounding the phenomenon are very different. In developing countries, UNICEF policy (for example) broadly speaking discourages early pregnancies on grounds of maternal and infant mortality and morbidity, maternal and infant nutrition and education, and of course on demographic grounds.

[2] For evidence of the relation between teenage fertility and socio-economic disadvantage, see Smith (1993), Jacobson et al (1995), Kiernan (1995, 1997). Kiernan, for example shows that 92% of the teenage mothers in the National Child Development Study (NCDS) had left school at 16 (for most of them this would have been *before* pregnancy), compared to 68% of women who became mothers between the ages of 20 and 33. Teenage mothers were also around twice as likely to have fallen into the bottom quartile when ranked on educational achievement at age 7 and 16, and considerably more likely to be from families which had experienced financial difficulties during their childhoods.

[3] For example Geronimus and Korenman (1992) and Hoffman et al (1993) find a reduced but still significant difference in outcomes for teenage mothers and those for their sisters who did not become pregnant: the mothers are less likely to complete high school and are likely to do less well in economic terms. But Hotz et al (1997) find teenage mothers earn *more* throughout their 20s than women who became pregnant as teens but miscarried. (Other studies from the US which draw attention to the problems of establishing causality are Geronimus, 1987, and Ribar, 1994.)

[4] Kiernan (1997) finds that 74% of teenage mothers in the NCDS claimed at age 33 that their first baby had been an accident. As she points out, this is likely to be an underestimate due to post hoc rationalisation.

[5] Under-16s in the UK can be prescribed contraception by their general practitioner without parental consent, but only at the doctor's discretion. Interviews in the surveys cited showed that many under-16s will not approach their doctors for fear that the doctor will tell the parents. In some cases, doctors themselves had refused to prescribe contraceptives without the permission of a parent (for example Sharpe, 1987, p 23; Allen, 1991, p 127).

[6] Bury (1984) and others cited in Phoenix (1991, p 46) claim pregnant teenagers of lower socio-economic status are more likely to continue with the pregnancy. Smith (1993) reaches the same result in a study of pregnant teenagers in Tayside, Scotland, in the 1980s.

[7] The causal impact of teenage birth on the life of mother and child may also, of course, be different.

[8] Throughout this chapter our data refer to the age of the mother at the birth of the child. Some sources use a different criterion – age at the end of the year in which the child is born (for example Social Exclusion Unit, 1999). This gives a substantially lower rate on account of the removal from the figures of mothers who were aged 19 at the birth of their child but who turned 20 in the year in question.

[9] For example, in the Netherlands, prescription costs for the pill, the IUD and the diaphragm have been covered by health insurance since 1971 (Jones et al, 1989, p 154); in 1974 free family planning services were made available nationwide in Britain (Jones et al, 1989, p 186), while in France women gained the right to claim contraceptives on health insurance and minors the right to free birth control without parental consent (Rodman and Trost, 1986, Chapter Six). Developments in Southern Europe were some way behind: in Italy in 1971 the law forbidding the advertisement of contraception was repealed and in 1975 the first family planning clinics were set up (Rodman and Trost, 1986, Chapter Nine). In Spain the law prohibiting the use of contraception was repealed in 1978 (Rodman and Trost, 1986, Chapter Ten).

[10] For example, more permissive abortion legislation was passed in the UK in 1967, in Denmark in 1973, in Sweden in 1975 and in the Netherlands in 1981. (In the latter two cases abortion had been widely available for some

years before the law was clarified). See Jones et al (1989) and Rodman and Trost (1986).

[11] Of course, miscarriage data would also be needed to put together a true conception rate, but births plus abortions should give a good picture of how conception rates vary across Europe since miscarriages can be expected to be proportional, broadly speaking, to this total.

[12] See Cossey (1997). In 1995 non-resident women accounted for 6% of abortions in England and Wales, mostly from Northern Ireland, the Republic of Ireland and France.

[13] Even among 13-15 year olds in the UK, the birth rate at the start of the 1990s was as high as 0.5% (5 per 1,000), and the conception rate 1% (CSO, 1994, chart 2.25); the latest figures for 1995-96 show the same levels (*The Guardian,* 12 December 1998).

[14] One illustration of the different ways in which sexual issues are treated in the two countries was given recently by a UK journalist: when AIDS first arrived, Dutch television demonstrated how to use a condom on prime-time television; in Britain the highly cryptic public service announcement centred around an iceberg (Toynbee, 1998).

[15] In 1985 the High Court in Britain ruled that girls under the age of 16 could not be prescribed contraception without parental consent, after a case brought by Victoria Gillick, mother of five girls under the age of 16. The ruling was later overruled by the Law Lords but is believed to have had a permanent effect on the freedom with which doctors discuss contraception with young teens and on the confidence teenagers have in asking family doctors for advice – it remains the case, for instance, that a doctor can breach confidentiality if she or he does not consider an underage girl to be of mature judgement (see Jones et al, 1986, p 110; Schofield, 1994, pp 20-2). A second significant event in Britain was the passage in 1988 of legislation designed to ensure that parents, not schools, should decide what constitutes appropriate sex education for their children (Phoenix, 1991, p 20). See also Toynbee (1998).

[16] The report includes a review of the evidence that availability of council housing and state benefits promotes teenage pregnancy in the UK, concluding that this is an "unprovable assertion" (Social Exclusion Unit, 1999, p 31).

SEVEN

Life satisfaction

This book has so far explored a variety of objective measures of child well-being. But what do children themselves say if asked about their welfare? In Europe a unique source allows us to investigate, if not the attitudes of younger children, at least what teenagers (aged 15-19) say for themselves about how happy they are. Eurobarometer surveys have been carried out twice annually in the EU member states since 1973, asking questions about public attitudes and opinion[1]. The question we focus on here is about life satisfaction: 'On the whole, are you very satisfied, fairly satisfied, not very satisfied, or not at all satisfied with the life you lead?' This question has been asked regularly since the survey began, allowing us to reach some conclusions about convergence in the way young people across Europe see their own quality of life[2].

The use of this kind of subjective information on well-being is somewhat controversial: although it has had a long history in the psychology literature, economists have tended to avoid it, perhaps because it does not sit well with the traditional view that utility cannot be directly measured[3]. However, there are good reasons to believe that what people say about their own welfare is interesting and important. Obviously it is not the only aspect of welfare we are interested in: there is cause for concern about someone who is malnourished, for instance, even if they claim to be happy with their situation. But it seems equally clear that life satisfaction is one important element of well-being. Echoing Sen on mortality (see Chapter 4) we might argue that being happy is, first, of intrinsic value in itself, and second, a prerequisite for participating fully in many other aspects of life[4]. And if we are interested in how happy someone is, asking them seems the most straightforward way to get the answer[5].

If rare, the use of subjective data is not unheard of among economists – and of course has been widely used by other social scientists. In the early 1970s, Easterlin used self-reported happiness levels to explore the relationship between national income and welfare (Easterlin, 1974). More recently, both Clark and Oswald (1994) and Wottiez and Theeuwes

(1998) have used surveys on subjective well-being to ask questions about labour market status and welfare, and in particular to look at the hypothesis that unemployment is voluntary. Nor indeed are we the first to use the Eurobarometer surveys to investigate the well-being of the young: Blanchflower and Oswald (1997) use the same data to look at the welfare of the under-30s.

Blanchflower and Oswald's results show a significant increase in life satisfaction among the young between the 1970s and the 1990s. However, their work focuses on this general rise and on possible explanations of it; they are not particularly interested in differences in happiness levels across countries. (They also use a broad definition of the young in contrast to our own focus on teenagers.) Of course, trying to compare results across countries leads to immediate problems: 'satisfaction' may be interpreted differently in different places for both linguistic and cultural reasons. Assuming, however, that the question is interpreted in the same way in a given country over time, then comparing national trends *is* informative. For instance, if the share of the young claiming to be happy has risen more in one country than in another over the last two decades, that tells us something even if the happiness levels themselves are not comparable in any one year.

A second issue of interest is how happy the young are relative to the rest of the population, and how this has changed over time. Suppose the population taken as a whole is increasingly satisfied with life. Are teenagers sharing equally in the phenomenon, or are they being excluded? Hence we look at trends in the ratio of youth satisfaction rates to those of the general population. These too should be unaffected by national differences in the way in which the question is interpreted.

Life satisfaction among the young (1975-94)

In keeping with the findings of Blanchflower and Oswald for the under-30s, life satisfaction among 15-19 year olds seems to be broadly on the rise across Europe. The share of this age group classifying themselves as 'very satisfied' or 'fairly satisfied' with their lives was significantly greater in the early 1990s than in the late 1970s in six of the EU 9 for which data are available for both periods[6,7]. Furthermore, in one of the exceptions, Denmark, progress could hardly have been expected: a striking 98% of young people declared themselves satisfied in the 1970s. The UK is a second exception: satisfaction levels fell slightly during the 1980s but have since recovered to the levels of the late 1970s. Only Belgium has seen the share of the young claiming to be satisfied fall over the period. In 1975-79, 94% of young Belgians put themselves in the top two satisfaction groups while in 1990-94 only 89% did so, a difference that is statistically significant at much better than the 1% level[8].

This in turn has led to convergence in the level of satisfaction across countries, as the share of the young who are basically happy with their lives grows towards 90% and beyond, as illustrated in Figure 7.1 (measures of dispersion are calculated for the EU 9 only). Progress has been particularly striking in Italy, where the share of young people claiming to be satisfied has risen steadily from just 62% in the 1970s to 87% in the early 1990s.

Figure 7.1: Percentage of 15-19 year olds 'very' or fairly' satified with their lives, selected EU countries

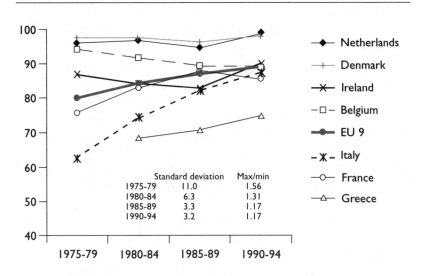

Source: Table E1

While, unfortunately, full data series are not available for the other Southern European countries, the evidence which does exist suggests that this Italian story may reflect something of a regional trend for southern Europe. Data for Greece are available for the last three periods and suggest a similar low starting point followed by improvement that was steady, though far less dramatic than in Italy (the increase is still significant at the 1% level if taken across the full period). For Spain and Portugal only the last two data points are available: Portugal records a significant rise of 80% to 87% across the five-year period (very similar to that in Italy over these years), but the Spanish rate remains stable at

84% to 85% in both years. By the 1990s, the difference from the average share of the young who are satisfied in the EU as a whole is small in Italy, Portugal and Spain, while Greece remains a notable outlier.

As Figure 7.1 shows, however, the rise in well-being has not been monotonic in all countries where increases have occurred. The fall in the satisfaction level in Ireland between the late 1970s and late 1980s is significant at the 1% level. (A similar decline was observed for the UK over the same period, but this is not significant.) This put Ireland and Belgium together on a downward trend at this time, in contrast to the course followed in the rest of Europe. However, in the 1990s both Ireland and the UK see a reversal of this trend: in Ireland in particular, the share of satisfied teenagers jumped by 6 percentage points over the last five-year period (the increases for both Ireland and the UK are statistically significant). The Belgian decline has continued. (The slight decline observed for France in the early 1990s in Figure 7.1 is not significant.[9, 10])

Do these aggregated figures for all young people hide a gender gap in life satisfaction? Pooling samples across the full 20 years, we find significant differences between results for boys and girls in only four countries. In three, a slightly higher share of boys than girls were found to be satisfied with their lives: 73% against 69% in Greece, 79% against 75% in Italy, and 97% against 95% in the Netherlands. In just one country, Ireland, a significantly higher share of the pooled sample of girls than boys claimed to be satisfied, but again the difference is small – 87% against 85%.

However, if numbers for each five-year period are looked at separately, one additional point of interest emerges: it is satisfaction levels among boys alone which is driving the rising aggregate level in Greece. In the early 1980s there was no significant difference between the share of boys (70%) and girls (67%) who said they were satisfied. But during the course of the decade, satisfaction among Greek boys increased to 79%, while among girls it rose just slightly to 69%. Greek girls appear not to be sharing the general rise in satisfaction levels in Europe[11].

Satisfaction among the young compared to the general population

How does the life satisfaction of young people compare with that of older groups? Do the improvements illustrated above reflect a trend shared by the whole population, or is the *relative* well-being of the young also improving? It turns out that the young are more likely than the general population to classify themselves as satisfied in almost every country, as illustrated in Figure 7.2, which plots the percentage of the young who claim to be satisfied with their lives against the percentage of the whole population (15-64) for 1990-94. The data points fall below the 45 degree line if a higher share of the young than of the general population declare themselves as satisfied; in practice all points fall along or below the line. The gap is particularly large where levels of satisfaction are lower, that is, in Greece, Spain, France, Portugal and Italy.

Furthermore, the gap between the two series has been increasing over time, as shown by the summary statistics given in Figure 7.2 for the ratio between the two (EU 9 only). The mean ratio has increased slightly: this is basically because satisfaction levels have stayed fairly constant among the total population and risen among the young, particularly in countries where satisfaction started low. The increase in the standard deviation is explained by the same phenomenon: as satisfaction increases, the young leave the older further behind in Southern Europe and France; while in countries with higher satisfaction levels to begin with (Denmark, Germany, Luxembourg and the Netherlands) there is little difference between the two series. There is certainly no story here of growing exclusion of the young, or of disparities between the young and the rest of the population across the EU changing in a way that is an obvious cause for concern. (If there is any concern, it is with the happiness of *adults* relative to children in Southern Europe.)

Figure 7.2: Percentages of 15-19 and 15-64 year olds 'very' or 'fairly' satisfied with their lives (1990-94)

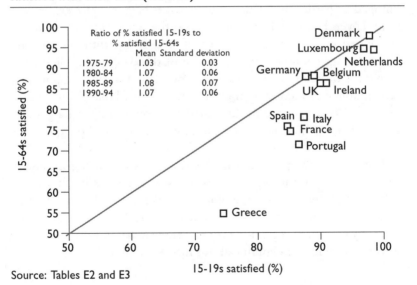

Source: Tables E2 and E3

Summary

To sum up, Europe has seen growing convergence in life satisfaction among young people, largely driven by increasing levels of satisfaction in Southern Europe, and particularly in Italy. The trend in Spain and Portugal looks likely to have been similar to that in Italy, but young people in Greece – and most strikingly Greek girls – remain some way behind.

These results suggest that life satisfaction data do pick up on an area of welfare not reflected by other indicators, although what exactly it is that is measured is hard to pinpoint. Blanchflower and Oswald put forward increasing personal and marital freedom as the cause of the growing well-being they identify among European under-30s: they show that it is predominantly young single people who are becoming happier, implying that in the past young people were constrained by their inability to postpone marriage or choose alternative life-styles. Clearly marital freedom is not the issue among the younger group we look at here, but the related idea of growing personal freedom could be of importance. The liberalisation of attitudes which have led to the postponement of marriage will have affected adolescents too.

A more obvious theory is that increasing satisfaction is simply the result of growing wealth in these countries. In fact rising wealth and liberalisation are likely to come hand in hand, and there may also be direct links between the two. For instance, increasing GDP in Southern Europe has given the young much greater access to their own transport – mopeds in particular – which in turn has enabled them to seize greater control over their own lives than was ever the case before. (This idea of the moped as the harbinger of liberty, if there is any truth in it, presents an interesting counterbalance to some of the dangers highlighted in Chapter 4 on road death rates. The rise of motorised transport may have inhibited the actions of the child and increased road deaths among teens but at the same time furnished the young with a heightened independence which has had a profound impact on their quality of life.)

The other story presented in this chapter is a growing malaise in some countries of the North. This is best exemplified by the case of Belgium, but Ireland also experienced a significant decline in the share of teenagers claiming to be satisfied during the 1980s. While satisfaction appears now to be rising among young people in Ireland, the continuing downward trend in Belgium calls for further attention.

Notes

[1] The Eurobarometer Surveys are organised by the European Commission. Samples of the population between the ages of 15 and 64 are interviewed in each survey. (The sample has a multistage probability design in some countries and a stratified quota design in others.) With data grouped across five-year intervals, reasonable sample sizes are obtained for the 15-19 age group – between 500 and 1,500 persons per country (with the exception of Luxembourg). (See Appendix Table E1.) Unfortunately, however, surveys are only carried out in EU member states, meaning they cover the EU 9 since the beginning and Greece, Spain and Portugal only since the early to mid-1980s. Data on Austria, Finland and Sweden are only available for 1994 and are not analysed here.

[2] Unfortunately the question was discontinued in 1995.

[3] Argyle (1989) is often cited as a readable introduction to the psychology literature (Clark and Oswald, 1994; Blanchflower and Oswald, 1997).

[4] It is perhaps harder to argue that life satisfaction is a proxy for other, harder to measure, variables (Sen's third justification for looking at mortality) although to the extent that this is true the case for using data on self-reported satisfaction is further strengthened.

[5] Indeed the only way? Other possibilities might be to measure how many times an individual smiles or laughs, or to ask others to rate a person's happiness. Blanchflower and Oswald (1997, p 1) cite evidence that self-reported levels of well-being are in any case correlated with these ratings.

[6] We chose to group these two categories together to try to minimise national differences in how the question is understood. There should be less difference across countries in the perception of the central dividing line between the two categories of 'satisfied' and the two of 'not satisfied' than in the interpretations of the words 'very' and 'fairly'. Note also that since our main interest is in trends over time, any fixed national differences in the way the question is understood by respondents are of less concern.

[7] The rise in the share of responses in the two categories was significant in each of these six countries on a Chi-squared test at the 1% level in every case (and often at much more demanding levels).

[8] The Chi-squared value was over 14. Results are calculated using weights provided in the dataset to ensure that the Walloon and Flemish populations of

Belgium are proportionately represented; hence there is no reason to believe that this result is due to a change in the sampling of the two groups.

[9] It should be noted that these results do not fit completely with those of Blanchflower and Oswald (1997) for the under-30s. Looking at the decade between 1983 and 1992 they find "a positive and statistically significant upward time trend over the most recent decade of 1983 to 1992 ... in each nation except Great Britain and Northern Ireland" (p 9). We do not find a significant upward trend for the UK, as noted, but we also have no evidence of an upward trend for Belgium, over any period (it is unlikely that this difference in findings is driven by the earlier cut-off point, 1992, used by Blanchflower and Oswald). It appears that teenagers in Belgium have been following a different – and less positive – trend than that followed by their compatriots in their 20s.

[10] The share of teenagers declaring themselves 'not at all' satisfied with their lives was also examined, to explore the possibility that the increasing numbers of satisfied teenagers detract attention from a growing minority of the very excluded. Results tell a very similar story to that already given. The share of the very unsatisfied has fallen in all of the EU 9 except Belgium and the UK, and in the latter two both the level and the increase are small and the change is unlikely to be significant (in 1990-94 under 3% put themselves in this group in both countries). Italy has experienced considerable improvement to match that illustrated above: in 1975-79 10% of teenagers said they were 'not at all' satisfied, falling to 2% by 1990-94. (These figures are still compatible with the rising youth suicide rates discussed in Chapter 4 because suicide is sufficiently rare: even in Finland in 1994 only 0.05% of the male population 15-24 died from suicide.) We also looked at the responses to a separate question on happiness, available for 1975-79 and 1982-86. (Respondents could classify themselves as 'very happy', 'fairly happy' or 'not too happy'; we combined the first two categories.) The pattern of responses across countries and the changes over time gave a very similar picture to that given by responses to the satisfaction question. (For example, the changes over time in happiness and satisfaction had a correlation of 0.81.)

[11] Only three other countries have significant gender differences in satisfaction levels for any one of the four periods taken separately: the Netherlands in 1980-84 with boys on 99% and girls on 94%; Ireland in the same period with boys on 81% and girls on 87%; and Luxembourg in 1990-94 with boys on 95% and girls on 99.7%.

EIGHT

Summary and conclusions

> Indicators for tracking the well-being of children and their families
> are important tools of government. Uses include simple description;
> monitoring to inform planning and resource allocation; goal-setting
> to guide broad policy and co-ordinate efforts across agencies and
> between levels of government; accountability efforts to hold agencies
> and even whole levels of government responsible for making progress
> toward specific social goals; and, under limited circumstances,
> evaluation of comprehensive government initiatives. (Brown, 1998,
> p 1)

The goal of closer integration in Europe requires the monitoring of
various aspects of the integration process. This is true not only of
macroeconomic performance, but also of living standards and the quality
of life – which are the real target of any new policy initiative at the
European level. Our aim in this book has been to investigate whether
the well-being of children in the different member states has become
more or less similar over time, and hence to contribute to the analysis of
economic and social cohesion in the European Union.

Strengthening cohesion in the Union means ensuring that "neither
regional location nor social position are permitted to circumscribe life-
chances" (European Commission, 1996, p 115) and a natural group to
focus on in this context is children. Moreover, children are a group
where pan-European support for action is likely to be high; it is not for
nothing that the UN Convention on the Rights of the Child has been
one of the most widely supported international human rights instruments
of all. And the Convention places considerable stress on economic and
social rights of children in domains of well-being measured by the data
we consider in this book.

What convergence in child welfare in the EU could actually mean
in practice is some startling improvements in the quality of life – we
noted, for example, that deaths among children under 5 years of age
would be reduced by about 10,000 a year if all member states were to

converge on the under-5 mortality rate of the best performer. On the other hand, we emphasised that convergence need not be a good thing – converging on the level of the poorer performers is certainly not desirable.

We first summarise our results and then highlight the need for further analysis and collection of data on European children.

Summary of results

As noted by the *First report on economic and social cohesion*, integration "should be about the quality of European citizenship in all its facets" (European Commission, 1996, p 46). The facets of child well-being we have looked at are only a sub-set of those that one would wish to consider (a point we return to below) but their range is sufficiently large that it would be surprising if all the indicators we have chosen were to move in the same way over time.

We have also emphasised that results can depend in part on the measuring rod chosen. The definitions of 'disparity' and of 'convergence' are not trivial issues; even the way that an indicator is expressed (for example 'mortality' versus 'survival') or whether the data for each country are weighted to account for differences in population size may be important for the conclusion drawn.

However, despite these difficulties, some clear and robust results do emerge from the analysis. In addition to GDP per capita, there is firm evidence of convergence (over varying time periods) on five indicators:

- Under-5 mortality
- Child traffic death rates
- Education expenditure as a share of GDP
- Enrolment in education at 16
- Life satisfaction

Of the remaining five indicators, three show divergence:

- Child poverty rates
- Worklessness among households with children
- Youth unemployment as a share of the cohort

And two show stagnation in terms of disparities:

- Male youth suicide rates
- Teenage fertility rates

These results relate to a measure of absolute disparity, the standard deviation, with measures weighted for differences in population size. Do the conclusions depend on these particular choices?

The five indicators that are found to converge with a measure of absolute disparity do so with a relative measure (the coefficient of variation), and with a measure that gives equal weight to all member states irrespective of their different sizes. The choice of measure makes little difference to results.

The five indicators which do *not* converge using the weighted standard deviation are more sensitive to the choice of convergence measure. If the weighted coefficient of variation is used, youth unemployment and (to a lesser extent) child poverty show stagnation or divergence – here there is little or no change in the picture; but the worklessness and youth suicide rates show convergence. However, this is convergence against a *worsening* average – that is, it is 'negative convergence'. Teenage fertility, on the other hand, shows divergence (rather than just stagnation), but this might be termed 'positive divergence' – divergence but against the background of an improving level of average well-being (lower fertility). In none of these three cases, then, is the picture given by the weighted standard deviation a misleading one in the sense that the indicator converges positively when we switch to the alternative measure.

If an unweighted measure is used, it is usually the degree rather than the direction of change in disparities which is affected. The two measures most affected are the youth suicide rate, where unweighted measures show divergence over the last decade rather than just stagnation, because of the greater impact of rising suicides in Finland; and the teenage fertility rate, where the opposite is the case. The failure of the UK teen fertility rate to converge has less impact on the unweighted figures as the UK is one of the EU's largest countries: the weighted standard deviation is more or less stagnant, while the unweighted standard deviation falls.

Results are fairly robust then to the choice of disparity measure used, and we find that half of our indicators show convergence while half show divergence or stagnation. Is there any pattern to be found which explains the division between converging indicators and those which do not converge? It is noteworthy that several of the measures which do converge might be thought of as standard indicators of the Human Development Index type – those chosen if measures of health status and education are used to supplement income-based measures so as to give us a more complete picture of human well-being. Child mortality rates and the expenditure and enrolment measures of education performance turn out to give a very similar picture of change in welfare to that provided by per capita GDP. On our measures of health and education status as well as our proxy for average income, child well-being is both improving and converging across the EU.

On the other hand, the indicators which tell us more about exclusion – about whether *all* children are benefiting from general progress overall – tend to tell a different story of falling standards and increasing disparities. The share of the young excluded from rising economic fortunes, as measured by child poverty rates, worklessness and youth unemployment rates, has been growing, and disparities across countries have also been increasing. The teenage fertility rate can also be thought of as an economic exclusion measure – although here convergence has been prevented by just one country, and average rates have fallen (welfare has risen). But youth suicide rates across Europe are higher than in 1970, while disparities have not fallen since 1985.

An argument could perhaps be made, then, that on average children's quality of life (measured in several dimensions) is on the rise across Europe, but that the risks of being excluded from improvements are also on the rise, and that these risks are becoming increasingly different across countries.

However, there is one exception to this rather disturbing picture – the data on life satisfaction. Despite falling welfare and rising disparities in all other 'exclusion' measures, a growing share of young people across Europe declare themselves to be satisfied with their lives. Of course, it should be remembered that only 15-19 year olds were asked for their opinion – we do not know that today's younger children would say the same thing, or that they will be as positive ten years down the line. Also, the phenomenon of rising spirits cannot be found everywhere: in Ireland and the UK the share claiming to be satisfied fell during the 1980s, and this decline has only been reversed in the last five years; in Belgium the share of satisfied young people is still falling. But it remains striking that in Italy, for instance, while youth unemployment rose from 13% to 17% between 1979 and 1994 (the figures relate to all individuals in the age range concerned), the satisfaction rate rose from 62% to 87% of 15-19 year olds. The satisfaction data suggest that exclusion indicators may in some cases be painting an overly negative picture of what is taking place.

It is worth pointing out that it is not always the same countries which are responsible for rising or persistent disparities (although one or two countries do stand out as having particularly bad records). This is in contrast to the situation among indicators which *have* converged, where the story reflects that of convergence in GDP per capita: broadly speaking, this is one of rapid catch-up progress by the Cohesion Four; or, more accurately, the Cohesion 'Three' – Greece, Spain and Portugal – often joined by Italy. (Child traffic death rates prove the exception: rates in Southern Europe have never reached those of Germany, Luxembourg, Denmark or Finland at their peaks, and convergence has been driven by progress in these latter countries.)

With measures which have not converged the story is less straightforward. Relationships are complex between different aspects of the welfare of even a single age group. Not all the countries with the highest levels of worklessness have high child poverty rates, for instance, while there is no cross-country correlation in our data between the youth unemployment rate and the youth suicide rate.

Sweden, Denmark and the Netherlands are found to have consistently good records on all indicators, while the UK, Ireland and Spain frequently number among the worst performers in the areas of no convergence. Germany has a worsening child poverty rate but an improving record on both youth unemployment and youth suicide; while the situation in Finland is the mirror opposite.

Finland and Ireland are unusual in that they have seen both their youth unemployment and youth suicide rates worsen with respect to the average: in general it is countries in Southern Europe which are doing badly on unemployment while suicide has risen most sharply in the North. However, despite better records on employment, family worklessness is highest in northern countries, especially in the UK, Ireland and Belgium. In the South, only Spain has unemployment high enough to bring family worklessness close to Northern levels.

In general, the Cohesion Three have a mixed record on these non-converging indicators. All three countries appear to have high child poverty rates. Youth unemployment and family worklessness are both high and rising in Spain. Greece and Portugal have low, stable levels of worklessness, and Greece and Spain consistently low rates of suicide. But in Greece youth unemployment has remained above the EU average since 1983; while Portugal has the second highest teenage fertility rate in Europe, and the highest rate of death from suicide and unexplained injury in the South.

In some cases we have been able to provide some explanation for the observed trends and hence some links to discussion of policy. But our main aim has been a more modest one, namely the documenting of 'what has happened to children' in Europe in the recent past. This forms the vital first step for the discussion of policy that can follow.

How did country X manage to reduce its child mortality rate faster than other countries at the same level of national income? Why has country Z diverged on teenage fertility? Differences in national policy affecting children and their families may well of course be only part of the explanation for the cross-national variation in outcomes. But observing those outcomes and lining countries' records over time up against each other is an important part of the policy process.

Finally, it should be noted that our results relate only to the differences between countries. But the differences *within* countries are also important for any analysis of cohesion. This is true not just from the national perspective but also from a European standpoint. The notion of solidarity within Europe does not imply indifference to a situation of wide disparities in living standards at the national level and it is worth noting that the *First report on economic and social cohesion* pointed to evidence of weakening social cohesion within some member states (European Commission, 1996). The report contained detailed analysis of incomes and employment at the level of the region, a unit of analysis on which EU policy has increasingly focused. The indicators of child well-being that we have considered in this book could usefully be analysed below the national level to see how sub-national differences (by region or social group) are changing over time.

Collection and analyis of data on children

Besides the substantive findings, our attempts to monitor children's well-being over time in a number of dimensions leads to conclusions about data sources and their analysis. In short, there is much scope for improvement. There are numerous dimensions of child welfare that one might wish to monitor over time in Europe, but which cannot be studied for lack of available data. The researcher's plea for more data is of course a familiar refrain but in this case we believe that it is warranted. Only in this way will children become "more visible ... which will make it possible to identify their needs and the issues which require priority political action" (Council of Europe, 1996, Article 6ii). The future of Europe lies with Europe's children and data collection and analytic efforts should match this reality.

The distinction between collection and analysis is an important one. On some issues, the required data do in general exist – child poverty, for example. The problem here is one of analysis. Work needs to be done to calculate and present child poverty rates from the existing household data sets on a regular basis and in a consistent fashion across countries.

Children need to be made a priority when the choice is made of the list of topics or population sub-groups to be analysed in the European Community Household Panel (ECHP), for example[1].

On other issues, however, the data need to be collected or made more widely available. The latter is especially relevant for an entity such as the EU, and the role of Eurostat, the Union's statistical agency, in bringing together and publishing comparable data for member states is of obvious importance here. As we noted, Eurostat has some very useful publications that present data on children (especially older children). But there are too many subjects for which data have to be obtained from other international organisations, or for which a time-consuming search through national sources must be undertaken (with all the problems of lack of comparability that this often entails). A regular Eurostat publication which focused on trends in different dimensions of child well-being would be a big step forward. The need for *regularity* in analysis and publication should be stressed. One-off publications do not provide for regular monitoring and allow issues to recede into the background.

Part of the data in such a publication would have to be collected afresh, or assembled from national sources; we are not advocating something that would merely be along the lines of what has been possible in this book. Some new subjects that need to be covered relate directly to key developments in economic policy in Europe, for example monetary union – Atkinson (1998a) calls for child-centred price indices and unemployment rates (similar to the workless household rate in Chapter 3) so that the impact of the single currency on children can be adequately monitored.

The list of other subjects that would be candidates to be covered, relevant to other policies at European or national level, is clearly vast. (In the case of older children, some good examples are found in *Youth in the European Union*, Eurostat, 1997a). Besides some of the obvious choices that we have been able to cover in this book (such as various mortality rates or teenage fertility) it might include low birth weight, immunisation, nutritional status, blood lead levels, and early childhood education among younger children; smoking, alcohol and drug use, sexually transmitted diseases, and both perpetration and victimisation of serious violent crime among youth. (We offer these merely as examples.)

Two indicators that appeal to us in the light of the analysis in this book are (i) information on children's mobility and independence, as measured by method of journey to school (see Chapter 4), and (ii) data on children and young people's learning achievement and their ability to apply knowledge, as in the TIMSS and the OECD *International Adult Literacy Survey* (discussed in Chapter 5). The former reflects the view that measurement of children's welfare should be concerned with their quality of life *while children*, rather than focusing on their acquisition of skills and capabilities to be used later in life. The latter relates to this 'investment' aspect and is clearly relevant to a traditional view of economic and social cohesion in the EU that stresses employment and income opportunities.

Note

[1] The need for this is illustrated by Eurostat's published analysis of income distribution in the ECHP. Analysis of the Wave 1 data (Eurostat, 1997e) included figures for the percentages of all individuals below different poverty lines (various percentages of mean and median) in each member state and also the percentages of children beneath these lines. The analysis of the Wave 2 data (Eurostat, 1998b) contained data for all individuals only.

Appendix: Sources of data on child well-being in the European Union

General sources

Eurostat is the obvious place to start when looking for data on children in Europe. The Eurostat website is at http://europa.eu.int/en/comm/eurostat. The site itself contains little in the way of statistics, but it does have lists of available publications and databases, along with prices and order forms.

In addition to the Eurostat publications referred to in relevant sections below, it is worth mentioning the regular Eurostat newsletter, *Statistics in Focus*. This appears in nine sub-series, one for each of the main statistical themes covered by Eurostat; *Population and Social Conditions* is the series which was of most use for this book. Each sub-series has several issues per year, with each issue containing a roundup of the latest results from surveys, studies or analyses published regularly by Eurostat.

All EU member states have ratified the UN Convention on the Rights of the Child; the periodic reports that they submit to the UN Committee on the Rights of the Child (which monitors compliance with the Convention), along with the Committee's responses, provide a useful qualitative source of information on the situation of children. Reports and Committee observations for sessions from 1997 onwards can be downloaded from the website of the UN High Commission for Human Rights at http://www.unhchr.ch/html/menu2/6/crcs.htm.

A Economic well-being

For GDP per capita we drew on figures published by Eurostat (or by the European Commission) which have the advantage of being presented already in purchasing power standard (PPS) terms. The *Eurostat Yearbook '97* (Eurostat, 1997d), for example, gives figures for each year 1986-96.

Microdata from the European Community Household Panel (ECHP), the source for the figures on child poverty in Table 2.1, are now available for secondary analysis – see Eurostat (1999). Our figures for child poverty in the 1980s and 1990s are from the research by Bradbury and Jäntti (1999) which uses the household survey datasets in the Luxembourg Income Study (LIS), described at the LIS website, http://lissy.ceps.lu. (See also the appendix in Atkinson, 1998b.)

The earlier study of child poverty by Hagenaars et al (1994) for the late 1980s (which was commissioned by Eurostat) is based on household budget surveys for the then EU 12. This is a very rich source of information on poverty in Europe. Besides containing extensive analysis, some 200 pages of tables in the appendices provide detailed breakdowns of poverty among the population as a whole, and among children, persons of other ages, regions, and a range of socio-economic groups. For each country the appendix tables include head-counts, poverty gaps, and other indices of the severity of poverty – based on a variety of poverty lines and equivalence scales. Figures are given based on both income and expenditure.

The Hagenaars et al study provides information on child poverty in households with and without work at one point in time but the 1998 OECD *Employment outlook* was the source we used to analyse the change in workless households. Unlike Hagenaars et al, this source uses labour force surveys. These data are not available for secondary analysis from a single supplier. (Labour force surveys for some EU countries are, however, available for secondary analysis through the Luxembourg Employment Study, described at the LIS website given above.)

The annual OECD *Employment outlook* is an excellent source of information on a variety of labour market topics relating to children and young people and by its nature allows the EU countries to be compared with North America and other OECD member states. This was the source used for data on youth unemployment. Results from the EU Labour Force Survey (for example Eurostat, 1998c) are published annually and provide an alternative source of unemployment data for a shorter time-series. (The survey was first carried out in 1983, but methodology was changed in 1992.) The *Eurostat Yearbook '97* provides some information too.

B Mortality

The standard source for mortality data is the World Health Organisation (WHO). All the mortality data used in the paper are from WHO. (The total death rate for 15-24 year olds is taken from the UN *Demographic Yearbook* for different years, as these were more easily at hand when we decided to include this indicator, but the Yearbooks themselves use WHO data (for example UN, 1998, p 2).

WHO data are available in the following formats:

1 WHO Health for all *database*

This is a user–friendly database on key healthcare indicators, covering Eastern and Western Europe. The latest version of the database can be downloaded from the website of the WHO Regional Office for Europe, in Copenhagen (currently at www.who.dk/country/country.htm). The database includes standard mortality indicators such as life expectancy, infant and under–5 mortality and maternal mortality, as well as breakdowns of total deaths by main cause. However, there are no age breakdowns by cause of death.

There is also a version of *Health for all* available at www.who.int/ whosis/hfa which includes some countries outside Europe. However, this contains a much more limited number of indicators, and a less complete time–series.

2 WHO World Health Statistics Annuals

These are annual yearbooks published since 1963, giving numbers and rates of death by country, with breakdowns by age group, gender and cause of death. The detail provided is likely to be sufficient for many purposes, but there are disadvantages. Most obviously, the data are not computerised and need to be entered by hand. Second, each annual includes the most recent data submitted for each country, whatever the year. Thus data for a given country for 1990 might be found in the yearbook for 1991, for 1992, for 1993 or for 1994. (Belgian data for 1989 were included in the 1993 yearbook and 1990 data had still not been published in mid–1999.) Finally, the age breakdown is by 10–year groups, so we have breakdowns for 5-14 year olds and for 15-24 year olds, when sometimes it would be preferable to have five–year breakdowns.

3 WHO Mortality *database*

The raw data used to put the *World Health Statistics Annuals* together are now available in electronic format. These can be downloaded from www.who.int/whosis/mort/download.htm.

These files eliminate the need for manual data entry, while allowing the researcher to reach a very fine degree of detail. Numbers of deaths are given by age of individual, gender and detailed classification of cause of death. However, they are raw data files and need work before they can be used: data given are numbers rather than rates, along with population figures. The files are also very large to download: the database covers all parts of the world, and it is not possible to download separate files for particular countries (although a small degree of selection is possible with respect to time period).

On the other hand, the files appear to be well documented, and the initial investment into downloading and setting them up would pay off if much use was going to be made of the data. (Had the files been available when we started putting our data together we would have done this; by the time we became aware of them it no longer made sense to do so.)

C Education

For **enrolment and expenditure data**, UNESCO is the main source used in this book. Expenditure data were taken from the *UNESCO Statistical Yearbook 1997* (1997), and enrolment data downloaded from the UNESCO website (http://unescostat.unesco.org/database/Dbframe.htm).

Other regular publications worth looking at include OECD *Education at a glance* (1997b), and various Eurostat publications (*Key data on education in the European Union*, 1997b and *Education across the European Union: Statistics and indicators*, 1997g). All of these provide useful detail, but tend to give data for the most recent available year only, making it hard work to put together a time series – and in fact the Eurostat publications are new, so for the moment this cannot be done anyway. (*Education across the European Union* gives time-series for some data such as number of pupils, which in principle could be used with population data to put together enrolment rates.)

For this book we also drew on two one-off Eurostat publications: *Youth in the European Union: From education to working life* (1997a) and Issue No 15 of *Statistics in Focus: Population and social conditions* (1998a) which concentrated on education spending.

For data on **education standards**, there are currently two surveys to look at:

1   the IEA's TIMSS Study (Beaton et al, *Mathematics* [or *Science*] *achievement in the middle school years: IEA's Third International Mathematics and Science Study*, 1996a, or see the website of Boston College at http://timss.bc.edu/ for further details including how

to access the raw data, and for progress on the 1998/99 TIMSS Repeat);

2   the OECD's functional literacy studies (*Literacy, economy and society: Results of the first International Adult Literacy Survey*, 1995, and *Literacy skills for the knowledge society: Further results from the International Adult Literacy Survey*, 1997a).

Future rounds of both studies will allow analysis of trends in national performance over time, and in the case of the OECD study there will be information on a wider group of countries (only 11 countries, including several outside Europe, were covered in the results we refer to in Chapter 5). The OECD is also conducting an important long-term study of 15 year olds to complement the *International Adult Literacy Survey*. Results from this new PISA study (Programme of International Student Assessment) are due to come on stream in 2001. All EU member states are included. Information can be found about PISA at http://www.oecd.org//els/Pisa.

D Teenage fertility

For **birth rate** data for recent years, the best source for Europe is the Eurostat electronic *Demographic Statistics Database 1997*, available on CD ROM. This contains annual data for 1990 to 1995 on number of births by age of mother (single year breakdowns), and population data, so birth rates can be estimated. (We used births to women aged 19 and under as the numerator, and population aged 15-19 as the denominator.) The database also breaks down number of births to each age group by marital status.

For earlier years, Eurostat fertility data are available in the annual print publication *Demographic Statistics*. The 1990 edition contains data for the EU 12 from 1960-90 (again, numbers of births are given alongside population figures, so that birth rates can be calculated). The obvious disadvantage is that data have to be entered by hand. In addition, space limits the degree of detail available: for instance, no data are given regarding marital status of teenage mothers.

For countries outside Europe, the best source seems to be the UN *Demographic Yearbooks* (in print). These were used in this paper for data up to 1990 for new EU members Austria, Finland and Sweden. Each yearbook gives only the latest available year for each country, so putting a time-series together is time-consuming. And again, the degree of detail is limited: numbers of births are only given for under-15s and 15-

19s (not for each age separately), and no information on marital status is given.

One problem in comparing teen birth rates across countries is that some countries record the age of mother as the age at the end of the calendar year in which the child was born, rather than the age at the birth itself. This can make a difference to the birth rates of some 30%. Some adjustment based on the average ratio between the two rates in other countries is therefore required.

Abortion data with age breakdowns are not easy to find. The source used in this paper is the WHO *Health for all* database (see **Mortality** above), which includes the number of abortions to women under 20. However, datapoints are only available for some countries for some years: it was possible to put together one or two datapoints in the early 1990s for about 10 European countries, but a longer time-series was possible for only a very few.

E Life satisfaction

Life satisfaction data are taken from the Eurobarometer biannual surveys. There is now a cumulative dataset which covers 1973-92. We merged this with the four six-monthly surveys held since then which have included the question on life satisfaction (Spring and Autumn 1993 and 1994). Since then the question appears to have been discontinued. The Eurobarometer datasets are stored at the Zentralarchiv für Empirische Sozialforschung (ZA) in Cologne and at the Inter-University Consortium for Political and Social Research (ICPSR) in Ann Arbor, Michigan, and are available to all interested researchers for a charge. For further information on how to access them see the ZA website at http://www.za.uni-koeln.de/data/en/eurobarometer/index.htm.

F Population

For 1990 onwards the best source for population data for Europe is the Eurostat electronic *Demographic Statistics Database 1997* on CD ROM. This contains annual population data by gender and for each age group.

For countries outside Europe, and for all countries prior to 1990, population data by gender and for five-year age breakdowns can be found in the UN Population Studies print publication *The sex and age distributions of the world populations*. The 1995 revision (published 1996) is the most recent.

A Economic well-being

A1: GDP per capita at current market prices in purchasing power parity (PPS) terms as % of weighted EU 15 average

	1983	1988	1993	1996
Austria	107.6	102.1	110.4	107.5
Belgium	105.4	103.3	113.9	112.6
Denmark	108.6	108.0	112.3	115.2
Finland	100.7	103.0	91.6	93.1
France	113.4	110.1	109.4	106.4
Germany	116.5	115.3	108.3	108.3
Greece	61.9	58.9	64.6	64.9
Ireland	63.6	64.6	83.4	99.8
Italy	101.6	102.0	101.9	105.1
Luxembourg	131.9	139.3	165.0	168.9
Netherlands	102.7	99.2	104.3	104.7
Portugal	55.1	58.7	67.0	67.5
Spain	70.5	72.8	78.1	77.0
Sweden	112.3	110.9	98.8	97.2
UK	98.7	102.5	99.3	99.0
mean	96.7	96.7	100.6	101.8
mean (wt)	100.1	100.0	100.0	100.0
CV	0.228	0.228	0.230	0.229
CV (wt)	0.172	0.161	0.128	0.127
max/min	2.39	2.37	2.55	2.60
Cohesion 4 mean as % EU 15 mean (both weighted)	66.1	67.7	74.4	74.8
Real GDP per capita (1983=100.0)	100.0	115.7	125.3	133.9

Notes: [1]Weighted calculations use 1980 population totals for 1983-88, 1993 total for 1993 and 1995 total for 1996. (Results for the weighted mean for 1988-96 differ somewhat from those given in the source table.)

[2]The Cohesion 4 are Greece, Ireland, Portugal and Spain.

Source: 1983: European Commission (1996, Table 2, p 132) (figures given only as % of weighted EU 15 mean); 1998-96: *Eurostat Yearbook '97* (Eurostat 1997d, p 210). Real GDP figures from European Commission (1996, Table 4, p 133) and for 1996 from Eurostat 1997d, p 208) (not per capita)

A2: Child poverty rates in different sources (%)

	1	2	3
Survey	ECHP Wave 1	LIS surveys	Budget surveys
measure	income	income	expenditure
year	1993	mainly early 1990s	1987-89
poverty line	50% mean	50% median	50% mean
equiv scale	modified OECD	NSF	modified OECD
age group	0-15	0-17	0-16
Austria	-	5.6	-
Belgium	15.0	6.1	7.5
Denmark	5.0	5.9	3.5
Finland	-	3.4	-
France	12.0	9.8	16.6
Germany	13.0	11.6	13.6
Greece	19.0	-	15.9
Ireland	28.0	14.8	18.8
Italy	24.0	21.2	20.3
Luxembourg	23.0	6.3	12.7
Netherlands	16.0	8.4	4.2
Portugal	27.0	-	22.9
Spain	25.0	13.1	17.8
Sweden	-	3.7	-
UK	32.0	21.3	17.8
correlation with ECHP figures	1.00	0.72	0.73

Notes:

1 The years to which the data from Bradbury and Jäntti refer are as in Table A3 with the exception of Italy and the UK (both 1995). The data for countries not included in Table A3 are from 1987 (Austria and Ireland), 1989 (France), 1990 (Spain) and 1992 (Sweden).

2 The modified OECD scale is 1+0.5*adults+0.3*children. The NSF scale used by Bradbury and Jäntti is (adults+0.7*children)^0.85.

3 The unit of analysis in every case is the child, with children classified as poor according to equivalised household income or expenditure. The income unit is the household except in the LIS data for Sweden where it is the family.

Sources:

1 Eurostat (1997e, Figure 3) (figures only given to nearest integer)

2 Bradbury and Jäntti (1999, Table 2.3)

3 Hagenaars et al (1994, Appendix A3, Table A2.1) (country tables)

A3: Child poverty rates in the 1980s and 1990s (%)

	Years	1980s	1990s
Belgium	(85,92)	4.7	6.1
Denmark	(87,92)	6.0	5.9
Finland	(87,91)	4.0	3.4
Germany	(84,94)	7.4	11.6
Italy	(86,91)	12.9	14.2
Luxembourg	(85,94)	5.5	6.3
Netherlands	(87,91)	6.6	8.4
Sweden	(87,92)	4.6	3.7
UK	(86,91)	14.3	20.3
mean		7.3	8.9
mean (wt)		10.5	13.5
CV		0.48	0.59
CV (wt)		0.35	0.38
SD		3.51	5.24
SD (wt)		3.67	5.06
max/min		3.60	6.00

Notes:

1 The table shows the percentage of children living in households with equivalised income beneath 50% of the median.

2 Weighted figures use 1985 population aged 0-14 for the 1980s and 1990 population of the same age for the 1990s.

3 See Table A2 for other notes (including definition of the equivalence scale).

Source: Luxembourg Income Study (LIS) microdata analysed by Bradbury and Jäntti (1999) and the basis for their Figure 3.2

A4: Households with children aged under 15: % with no working adult

	1985	1996
Belgium	7.2	11.0
France	6.4	8.8
Germany	6.8	8.6
Greece	6.3	4.5
Ireland	17.2	15.4
Italy	3.5	7.6
Luxembourg	2.5	3.8
Netherlands	11.1	9.3
Portugal	3.8	3.3
Spain	8.3	10.1
UK	15.0	19.5
mean	8.0	9.3
mean (wt)	8.0	10.6
CV	0.56	0.50
CV (wt)	0.50	0.43
SD	4.47	4.64
SD (wt)	3.98	4.56
max/min	7.00	5.91

Note: Weighted figures use 1985 population aged 0-14 for 1985 and 1995 population for 1996.

Source: OECD (1998, Tables 1.6 and 1.7)

A5: Unemployment rates, 20-24 year olds

	1979	1983	1989	1994
Austria	–	–	–	–
Belgium	–	21.7	14.6	20.4
Denmark	–	17.7	13.5	12.6
Finland	7.8	8.2	5.5	30.2
France	10.9	17.3	19.1	27.7
Germany	4.3	11.7	6.8	8.9
Greece	–	21.4	24.1	25.5
Ireland	6.9	16.3	17.0	22.2
Italy	20.7	25.2	30.7	30.9
Luxembourg	–	5.0	1.9	6.3
Netherlands	–	17.2	11.0	10.1
Portugal	15.0	18.4	11.3	13.6
Spain	15.3	32.1	31.8	41.4
Sweden	3.7	6.8	3.1	16.6
UK	–	17.9	9.7	14.8
EU 14 (unweighted)		16.9	14.3	20.1

Source: OECD (1996, Table 4.3, p 114) (figures for each gender weighted using participation rates in Table 4.1, p 111). These unemployment rates relate to those 20-24 year olds participating in the labour force, in contrast to those in Table A7

A6: Labour force participation rates, 20-24 year olds

	1979	1983	1989	1994
Austria	–	–	–	–
Belgium	–	69.6	60.6	59.1
Denmark	–	84.5	84.3	76.5
Finland	75.3	76.8	76.0	64.8
France	74.5	73.4	64.6	51.9
Germany	75.6	74.8	75.9	73.2
Greece	–	63.2	63.0	59.8
Ireland	79.9	82.0	77.6	72.6
Italy	63.6	66.2	67.7	54.3
Luxembourg	–	77.3	73.1	68.5
Netherlands	–	73.0	75.1	75.2
Portugal	80.0	75.4	70.6	65.4
Spain	69.5	69.5	70.0	64.3
Sweden	81.8	82.4	82.6	65.8
UK	–	80.9	83.6	76.9
EU 14 (unweighted)	–	74.9	73.2	66.3

Source: OECD (1996, Table 4.1, p 111) (average of figures for each gender)

A7: Cohort unemployment rates, 20-24 year olds

	1979	1983	1989	1994
Austria	–	–	–	–
Belgium	–	15.1	8.8	12.0
Denmark	–	15.0	11.4	9.7
Finland	5.9	6.3	4.2	19.6
France	8.1	12.7	12.4	14.4
Germany	3.3	8.8	5.2	6.5
Greece	–	13.6	15.2	15.3
Ireland	5.5	13.4	13.2	16.1
Italy	13.1	16.7	20.8	16.8
Luxemb.	–	3.9	1.4	4.3
Netherl.	–	12.6	8.2	7.6
Portugal	12.0	13.9	8.0	8.9
Spain	10.6	22.3	22.2	26.6
Sweden	3.0	5.6	2.5	10.9
UK	–	14.5	8.1	11.4
EU 14 (unweighted)		12.4	10.1	12.9
EU 12 (weighted)		14.0	12.4	13.8
CV		0.33	0.49	0.44
CV (w)		0.30	0.52	0.44
SD		4.7	6.0	5.6
SD (w)				
max/min		5.73	15.59	6.14

Note: These unemployment rates relate to all 20-24 year olds, in contrast to those in Table A5 which are calculated as a percentage of those persons participating in the labour force. (Rates have been calculated separately for men and women and then averaged, which accounts for any small differences from those implied by Tables A5 and A6.)

Source: OECD (1996, Table 4.1, p 111 and Table 4.3, p 114)

B Mortality

B1: Under-5 mortality (probability of dying before age 5 per 1,000)

	1970	1975	1980	1985	1990	1995
Austria	29.8	23.8	17.0	13.3	9.6	6.7
Belgium	24.5	19.0	14.7	11.5	9.7	9.6
Denmark	16.9	12.5	10.4	9.5	8.9	6.3
Finland	16.2	12.6	9.1	7.4	6.7	5.0
France	18.3	16.5	12.3	10.1	8.9	7.1
Germany	27.4	22.9	15.1	10.7	8.5	7.1
Greece	33.4	26.8	20.3	15.8	10.9	9.0
Ireland	22.8	20.8	13.7	10.6	9.7	7.3
Italy	33.4	23.2	16.2	11.8	9.2	8.5
Luxembourg	24.7	15.7	12.5	10.6	8.8	4.4
Netherlands	16.0	13.4	10.7	9.7	8.7	6.8
Portugal	62.2	46.2	29.2	21.6	14.0	9.6
Spain	24.5	22.0	15.0	10.9	9.4	7.6
Sweden	13.1	10.3	8.3	7.9	7.1	4.7
UK	21.4	18.5	14.1	11.2	9.4	7.2
Mean (unweighted)	25.6	20.3	14.6	11.5	9.3	7.1
Mean (weighted)	25.8	20.8	14.9	11.3	9.2	7.5
CV	0.45	0.41	0.34	0.29	0.17	0.22
CV (w)	0.34	0.29	0.24	0.21	0.12	0.13
SD	11.5	8.4	4.9	3.3	1.6	1.6
SD (w)	8.9	6.0	3.6	2.3	1.1	0.9
max/min	4.8	4.5	3.5	2.9	2.1	2.2

Notes: 1970 figures for Portugal and Luxembourg are, in fact, 1971; 1995 figures are 1992 for Belgium, 1993 for Germany, Ireland and Italy, and 1994 for Spain. Until 1990 data for Germany are for FRG; 1990 and 1995 data are for united Germany. Weighted calculations use population data from Table F1.

Source: WHO (1998)

B2: Total death rate for 15-24 year olds (deaths per 100,000)

	1970	1975	1980	1985	1990	1995
Austria	115.9	109.8	108.0	93.5	76.8	72.7
Belgium	86.2	89.7	89.7	73.6	78.9	-
Denmark	73.6	70.7	75.7	66.5	54.8	56.1
Finland	94.6	102.3	74.0	68.0	92.8	60.4
France	100.6	100.0	103.7	85.1	76.9	74.6
Germany	121.5	105.9	90.1	66.3	70.4	61.8
Greece	67.1	68.3	64.9	70.8	69.6	63.5
Ireland	72.2	68.7	65.4	59.7	56.9	59.4
Italy	80.5	73.9	73.2	61.2	61.9	71.3
Luxembourg	127.7	141.5	81.2	100.0	82.5	76.8
Netherlands	76.2	61.5	60.2	49.2	44.7	44.3
Portugal	94.4	127.3	112.9	102.6	108.5	102.1
Spain	75.6	67.8	65.9	69.7	84.4	65.7
Sweden	73.9	74.8	57.7	54.6	53.2	39.3
UK	67.5	67.7	63.6	53.8	57.7	53.3
Mean (unweighted)	88.5	88.7	79.1	71.6	71.3	64.4
Mean (weighted)	88.5	84.9	80.2	67.7	69.6	65.0
CV	0.22	0.27	0.22	0.22	0.23	0.23
CV (w)	0.21	0.22	0.21	0.19	0.18	0.17
SD	19.3	23.8	17.3	16.1	16.4	14.8
SD (w)	18.8	18.3	16.6	12.7	12.5	11.3
max/min	1.9	2.3	2.0	2.1	2.4	2.6

Notes: Data for Germany and Sweden (1970) are for 1971; for Austria (1975) 1976; for Belgium and Spain (1985) 1986; for Belgium, Italy, Luxembourg and Spain (1990) 1989; for Italy (1995) 1992; for France and Spain 1993; and for Sweden 1994. Data for Germany are for FRG until 1985 inclusive; for united Germany for 1990 and 1995. No data for Belgium are available since 1989. Weighted calculations use population data from Table F6 (1995 population data used for 1994 calculations).

Source: Calculated from absolute numbers of deaths in UN Demographic Yearbooks and population data in Table F6. Data for 1970 are from UN (1972, pp 714-20), UN (1973, pp 550-6) and UN (1974, p 304). Data for 1975 are from UN (1981, pp 514-32); for 1980 from UN (1986, pp 566-86); and for 1985 from UN (1994, pp 550-70). Data for 1995 are from UN (1998, pp 576-98). Exception: figure for Belgium 1990 is from WHO (1994, p D-140)

**B3: Deaths from motor vehicle accidents among children aged 5-14
(deaths per 100,000)**

	1960	1965	1970	1975	1980	1985	1990	1994
Austria	8.4	9.7	12.2	12.0	6.1	6.5	4.0	3.4
Belgium	8.4	11.7	13.7	9.1	8.8	7.8	5.6	-
Denmark	8.2	13.3	17.1	12.1	4.2	8.7	6.8	4.4
Finland	10.6	13.0	14.8	9.4	4.6	6.7	5.2	4.7
France	–	8.3	8.2	6.5	6.7	5.3	4.3	3.4
Germany	11.2	13.4	17.3	10.6	8.8	5.2	4.0	3.2
Greece	2.7	4.8	3.4	5.3	5.9	5.7	6.6	4.7
Ireland	5.4	6.3	8.2	8.2	7.1	4.8	4.6	3.5
Italy	6.0	7.4	9.3	8.1	6.7	4.2	4.1	3.4
Luxembourg	–	8.2	15.7	3.9	8.2	7.1	7.0	4.3
Netherlands	9.1	11.1	13.3	9.3	7.4	4.2	4.5	3.7
Portugal	6.0	7.8	9.6	12.9	13.0	8.4	9.0	7.4
Spain	2.0	4.2	5.0	5.2	5.5	5.0	4.8	4.6
Sweden	8.5	9.6	9.2	7.6	5.3	3.6	2.6	1.9
UK	6.6	7.6	7.1	5.8	5.1	5.7	4.1	2.9
Mean (unweighted)	7.2	9.1	10.9	8.4	6.9	5.9	5.2	3.9
Mean (weighted)	7.2	8.7	10.1	7.9	6.8	5.3	4.5	3.6
CV	0.37	0.31	0.38	0.31	0.31	0.25	0.30	0.31
CV (w)	0.42	0.33	0.42	0.28	0.25	0.20	0.23	0.25
SD	2.6	2.8	4.2	2.6	2.1	1.5	1.6	1.2
SD (w)	2.9	2.9	4.2	2.2	1.7	1.1	1.1	0.9
max/min	5.7	3.2	5.1	3.3	3.1	2.4	3.4	3.9

Notes: Data point for Spain (1960) is for 1958; data for Ireland and Luxembourg
(1965) are for 1966; for Italy and Luxembourg (1975) 1974; for Belgium and Greece
(1980) 1979 and for France 1981; for Belgium (1985) 1984, (1990) 1989; for Spain,
Italy and Ireland (1994) for 1992 and for Denmark, France and Sweden 1993. Data
for Germany are for the FRG until 1990; data for 1990 and 1994 are for the united
Germany. No data for Belgium are available since 1989. Weighted calculations use
population data in Table F2 (1995 population data used for 1994 calculations).

Source: WHO (1966, 1967, 1968, 1972, 1973, 1974, 1977, 1978, 1979, 1982, 1983,
1984, 1987, 1988, 1989, 1992, 1993, 1994, 1995, 1996a)

B4: Traffic deaths for two groups of young males (1970 and 1994)
(deaths per 100,000)

| | 5-14 | | 15-24 | |
	1970	1994	1970	1994
Austria	16.5	5.0	85.2	56.4
Belgium	17.1	5.5	62.9	57.4
Denmark	19.5	4.2	45.4	25.1
Finland	20.3	6.4	41.9	23.2
France	9.6	4.0	47.0	42.5
Germany	21.7	3.6	84.9	39.8
Greece	4.9	5.0	22.4	54.1
Ireland	10.6	5.2	26.4	37.2
Italy	12.8	4.4	47.1	48.6
Luxembourg	19.2	4.2	135.8	40.0
Netherlands	18.3	4.1	51.7	19.0
Portugal	12.4	9.3	41.2	55.0
Spain	6.7	5.0	22.9	43.7
Sweden	12.3	1.7	36.5	16.7
UK	9.6	3.8	37.0	18.0
Mean (unweighted)	14.1	4.8	52.6	38.4
Mean (weighted)	13.0	4.3	49.0	38.8
CV	0.36	0.33	0.55	0.37
CV (w)	0.40	0.26	0.40	0.32
SD	5.1	1.6	28.8	14.2
SD (w)	5.2	1.1	19.4	12.2
max/min	4.4	5.5	6.1	3.4

Notes: 1994 data are for 1989 for Belgium; for 1992 for Spain, Italy and Ireland; and for 1993 for Denmark, France and Sweden. Data for Germany are for FRG for 1970 and for the united Germany for 1994. Weighted calculations use population data from Table F2 for the younger group (as a proxy for male population) and from Table F7 for the older group. 1995 population figures are used to weight 1994 mortality data.

Source: See Table B3

B5: Suicide rates among 15-24 year old males (deaths per 100,000)

	1970	1975	1980	1985	1990	1994
Austria	27.0	24.1	32.5	32.5	25.5	26.5
Belgium	8.8	14.3	14.8	18.7	20.2	–
Denmark	13.6	17.4	22.2	20.5	16.7	15.9
Finland	24.7	48.7	42.4	40.0	57.5	50.5
France	11.6	18.4	18.8	22.0	18.3	23.5
Germany	21.3	24.5	21.7	21.7	16.8	16.5
Greece	3.2	4.0	3.5	5.7	5.2	4.2
Ireland	6.8	9.7	8.9	17.8	16.1	23.4
Italy	4.0	3.4	5.5	6.3	6.7	7.6
Luxembourg	8.2	10.3	11.1	14.7	23.2	32.6
Netherlands	5.9	8.1	9.1	11.1	8.7	9.9
Portugal	7.3	5.6	14.3	20.9	23.9	15.8
Spain	2.0	2.3	4.4	8.5	8.0	7.1
Sweden	20.8	29.3	22.8	17.8	19.4	15.7
UK	7.6	10.0	10.7	12.8	18.2	18.5
Mean (unweighted)	11.5	15.3	16.2	18.1	19.0	19.1
Mean (weighted)	10.3	13.3	13.8	15.5	14.9	15.3
CV	0.68	0.78	0.65	0.50	0.63	0.61
CV (w)	0.69	0.72	0.58	0.48	0.49	0.49
SD	7.8	12.0	10.5	9.0	12.0	11.6
SD (w)	7.1	9.6	8.1	7.4	7.3	7.5
max/min	13.5	21.2	12.1	7.0	11.1	12.0

Notes: Datapoint for Spain (1960) is for 1958; data for Ireland and Luxembourg (1965) are for 1966; for Italy and Luxembourg (1975) 1974; for Belgium and Greece (1980) 1979 and for France 1981; for Belgium (1985) 1984; and for Belgium (1990) 1989. 1994 data are for 1992 for Spain, Italy and Ireland; and for 1993 for Denmark, France and Sweden. Data for Germany are for the FRG until 1990; data for 1990 and 1994 are for the united Germany. No data for Belgium are available since 1989. Weighted calculations use population data from Table F7 (1994 population data are used to weight 1995 mortality rates).

Source: See Table B3

B6: Deaths from suicide and unexplained violence for 45-54 year old males (deaths per 100,000)

	1970	1975	1980	1985	1990	1994
Austria	58.5	59.6	63.4	57.2	48.9	44.1
Belgium	32.8	29.7	41.8	44.8	33.6	–
Denmark	59.3	60.7	71.8	62.7	60.3	51.9
Finland	67.3	62.1	69.9	64.0	77.9	66.7
France	39.3	45.1	47.3	52.6	48.3	47.6
Germany	45.0	46.0	45.4	43.5	37.9	35.2
Greece	7.6	5.6	6.6	8.1	5.3	7.3
Ireland	8.7	14.8	28.1	14.5	26.8	22.5
Italy	12.2	9.9	14.3	16.2	12.2	14.5
Luxembourg	27.8	22.3	40.8	25.0	29.4	38.5
Netherlands	16.1	20.8	18.3	21.4	16.0	18.9
Portugal	14.5	24.8	32.6	40.9	38.1	28.6
Spain	9.6	9.4	9.8	17.2	13.2	13.5
Sweden	61.1	59.5	64.4	56.2	47.1	46.4
UK	17.7	19.2	20.5	23.8	24.1	20.9
Mean (unweighted)	31.8	32.6	38.3	36.5	34.6	32.6
Mean (weighted)	27.8	29.0	31.2	33.1	30.0	28.6
CV	0.66	0.62	0.56	0.51	0.55	0.51
CV (w)	0.60	0.61	0.57	0.48	0.51	0.49
SD	20.9	20.1	21.3	18.7	19.1	16.7
SD (w)	16.8	17.6	17.9	16.0	15.4	13.9
max/min	8.9	11.1	10.9	7.9	14.7	9.1

Notes: Datapoint for Spain (1960) is for 1958; data for Ireland and Luxembourg (1965) are for 1966; for Italy and Luxembourg (1975) 1974; for Belgium and Greece (1980) 1979 and for France 1981; for Belgium (1985) 1984; and for Belgium (1990) 1989. 1994 data are for 1992 for Spain, Italy and Ireland; and for 1993 for Denmark, France and Sweden. Data for Germany are for the FRG until 1990; data for 1990 and 1994 are for the united Germany. No data are available for Belgium since 1989. Weighted calculations use total populations in Table F8 as proxy for male population 45-54 (1995 population data used to weight 1994 mortality data).

Source: See Table B3

B7: Homicide deaths for young men aged 15-24 (deaths per 100,000)

	1970	1975	1980	1985	1990	1994
Austria	2.8	1.8	1.1	0.9	1.8	0.4
Belgium	0.8	0.9	1.7	1.7	1.4	–
Denmark	0.5	0.5	1.3	1.7	1.3	2.5
Finland	3.6	6.2	4.3	2.7	3.6	1.9
France	0.5	1.2	1.2	1.2	0.9	1.4
Germany	1.5	1.3	1.0	0.9	1.1	1.3
Greece	0.8	1.3	1.1	1.4	1.6	1.6
Ireland	0.4	1.5	1.0	0.6	0.6	1.9
Italy	1.0	2.1	3.2	2.9	4.9	4.4
Luxembourg	4.1	–	3.5	–	3.9	–
Netherlands	0.9	1.1	1.4	0.6	1.3	0.8
Portugal	5.6	5.5	1.6	2.0	2.4	1.8
Spain	0.6	1.2	1.7	2.0	1.2	1.3
Sweden	1.3	2.3	1.0	1.3	1.8	1.8
UK	1.3	3.2	1.6	1.3	1.5	2.1
Mean (unweighted)	1.7	2.2	1.8	1.5	2.0	1.8
CV	0.89	0.77	0.56	0.45	0.61	0.52
CV (w)	0.82	0.81	0.55	0.68	0.64	0.75
SD	1.5	1.6	1.0	0.7	1.2	0.9
SD (w)	1.5	1.3	1.1	0.9	1.5	1.3
max/min	14.0	12.4	4.3	4.8	8.2	11.0

Notes: Datapoint for Spain (1960) is for 1958; data for Ireland and Luxembourg (1965) are for 1966; for Italy and Luxembourg (1975) 1974; for Belgium and Greece (1980) 1979 and for France 1981; for Belgium (1985) 1984; and for Belgium (1990) 1989. 1994 data are for 1992 for Spain, Italy and Ireland; and for 1993 for Denmark, France and Sweden. Data for Germany are for the FRG until 1990; data for 1990 and 1994 are for the united Germany. No data are available for Belgium since 1989. Weighted calculations use population data in Table F7 (1995 population data used to weight 1994 mortality data).

Source: See Table B3

C Education

C1: Consolidated public education expenditure as a share of GNP (%)

	1980	1985	1990	1995
Austria	5.6	5.9	5.4	5.5
Belgium	6.1	6.2	5.1	5.7
Denmark	6.9	7.2	7.5	8.3
Finland	5.3	5.4	5.7	7.6
France	5.0	5.8	5.4	5.9
Germany	4.7	4.6	4.1	4.7
Greece	2.2	2.9	3.1	3.7
Ireland	6.3	6.4	5.7	6.3
Italy	4.4	5.0	5.4	4.9
Luxembourg	5.7	3.8	–	–
Netherlands	7.6	6.4	6.0	5.3
Portugal	3.8	4.0	4.3	5.4
Spain	2.6	3.3	4.4	5.0
Sweden	9.0	7.7	7.7	8.0
UK	5.6	4.9	4.9	5.0
Mean (unweighted)	5.4	5.3	5.3	5.8
Mean (weighted)	4.9	5.0	4.9	5.2
CV	0.32	0.26	0.22	0.22
CV (w)	0.27	0.20	0.17	0.15
SD	1.7	1.4	1.2	1.3
SD (w)	1.3	1.0	0.8	0.8
max/min	4.1	2.7	2.5	2.2

Notes: 1980 data are in fact 1979 for Greece, Italy and Spain; 1985 is 1986 for Luxembourg; 1990 is 1989 for Denmark; 1995 are 1994 for Belgium, Finland, France, Germany, Italy, Netherlands, Portugal, Spain and Sweden. Data for Germany for 1980 and 1985 refer to FRG; 1990 and 1995 to the united Germany. Except for 1995, Belgian data refer to expenditure of Ministry of Education only. Portuguese figure for 1990 refers to expenditure of the Ministry of Education only. French data refer to Metropolitan France.

Source: UNESCO (1997, Table 4.1) except for Germany and Italy (1990) and UK (1995) from Eurostat (1997d, p 240)

C2: Consolidated public education expenditure as a share of GNP, adjusted by share of population aged 5-24 (%)

	1980	1985	1990	1995
Austria	5.6	6.0	5.5	5.7
Belgium	6.3	6.6	5.3	5.9
Denmark	7.2	7.5	7.8	8.7
Finland	5.6	5.8	6.0	7.7
France	5.0	5.9	5.2	5.5
Germany	5.0	5.1	4.6	5.3
Greece	2.3	2.9	2.9	3.5
Ireland	5.2	5.1	4.3	4.6
Italy	4.4	4.8	5.4	5.1
Luxembourg	6.0	4.2	–	–
Netherlands	7.1	6.2	5.9	5.3
Portugal	3.4	3.6	3.8	4.8
Spain	2.4	2.9	3.8	4.5
Sweden	10.3	8.6	8.4	8.3
UK	5.7	5.0	5.0	5.0
Mean (unweighted)	5.4	5.3	5.3	5.7
Mean (weighted)	4.9	5.0	4.9	5.2
CV	0.35	0.29	0.27	0.26
CV (w)	0.30	0.24	0.18	0.16
SD	1.9	1.5	1.4	1.5
SD (w)	1.5	1.2	0.9	0.8
max/min	4.5	3.0	2.9	2.5

Notes: Let $A(i)$ = share of 5-24 year olds in EU population/share in population of country i (from Tables F2, F6, F8). Let $EDEXP(i)$ be education expenditure as a share of GNP in country i (from Table C1). This table then shows $A(i)*EDEXP(i)$. Weighted calculations use population of 5 to 24 from Tables F2 and F6.

Source: Education expenditure data from Table C1 above; adjusted by population data in Tables F2, F6 and F8

C3: Consolidated public education expenditure as a share of GDP, by level (1995) (%)

	Total	Primary	Secondary	Tertiary
Austria	5.8	1.2	2.9	1.1
Belgium	5.9	1.2	2.8	1.3
Denmark	8.4	1.8	3.4	1.9
Finland	7.4	1.7	2.6	2.5
France	5.6	1.1	2.8	1.1
Germany	5.4	–	3.9	1.3
Greece	2.7	1.2	1.1	0.7
Ireland	3.8	0.9	1.4	1.1
Italy	4.9	1.3	2.3	0.6
Luxembourg	4.8	2.2	2.1	0.2
Netherlands	5.2	1.1	2.2	1.6
Portugal	5.1	1.9	1.9	0.9
Spain	4.4	1.2	2.0	0.8
Sweden	8.1	1.9	3.3	2.4
UK	5.2	1.4	2.3	1.2
Mean (unweighted)	5.5	1.4	2.5	1.2
Mean (weighted)	5.2	1.0	2.7	1.1

Notes: Primary is defined as ISCED 1; Secondary as ISCED 2 and 3; and Tertiary as ISCED 5-7. Primary figure for Greece in fact shows ISCED 0 and 1; Secondary figure for Germany shows ISCED 0-3. Unweighted averages for primary and secondary education are calculated without Germany. Weighted averages are from original source. The data are adjusted for the share of the population aged 5-24 in the same way as the data in Table C2.

Source: Eurostat (1998a)

C4: Enrolment rates in secondary education for 16 year olds (%)

	1964/ 65	1969/ 70	1974/ 75	1979/ 80	1984/ 85	1989/ 90	1994/ 95
Austria	71	33	36	43	–	–	90
Belgium	56	63	70	77	85	89	100
Denmark	–	–	–	89	85	90	92
Finland	–	53	–	85	–	97	92
France	50	57	69	72	75	83	92
Germany	–	–	–	–	–	–	96
Greece	39	45	55	59	73	76	79
Ireland	42	55	63	70	83	87	91
Italy	31	52	51	51	–	–	–
Luxembourg	72	47	47	65	71	75	77
Netherlands	–	57	75	86	88	90	89
Portugal	19	22	36	38	–	68	78
Spain	17	27	45	54	–	–	89
Sweden	68	–	–	83	–	83	95
UK	29	–	58	44	54	57	82
Mean (unweighted)		48	58	65	73	80	88
Mean (weighted)		45	58	60	68	75	88
CV		0.31	0.25	0.26	0.18	0.14	0.08
CV (w)		0.31	0.21	0.25	0.17	0.15	0.06
SD		15.0	14.7	17.0	13.3	10.9	7.3
SD (w)		13.8	12.2	14.9	11.6	11.4	5.5
max/min		3.3	2.2	2.3	1.7	1.7	1.3

Notes: EU averages and dispersion measures are calculated for the 12 countries for which there is a continuous series, and on the basis of extrapolation of missing datapoints. Enrolment rates are for full-time education, including technical and vocational education. Data for 1964/65 are for 1965/66 for Ireland, Luxembourg and UK; for 1966/67 for Italy and for 1968/69 for Austria. Data for 1969/70 are for 1968/69 for Belgium. Data for 1974/75 are for 1975/76 in France, Italy and Portugal and for 1976/77 for Belgium. Data for 1979/80 are for 1977/78 in Portugal; for 1978/79 in Belgium, Finland and Italy; for 1980/81 in Denmark and the UK; and for 1981/82 in Sweden. Data for 1984/85 are for 1985/86 in Ireland, Luxembourg and the UK. Data for 1989/90 are for 1987/88 in Luxembourg; 1990/91 in Belgium and Finland; and 1992/93 in Portugal. Data for 1994/95 are for 1992/93 in the Netherlands; and for 1993/94 in Belgium, France and Portugal.

Source: UNESCO (1998b)

C5: Share of 16-24 year olds who claim to have left school after the age of 16 (%)

	Interview period (%)				Sample sizes			
	1975 -79	1980 -84	1985 -89	1990 -94	1975 -79	1980 -84	1985 -89	1990 -94
Belgium	76	77	86	94	2,051	1,908	2,163	1,431
Denmark	67	73	85	94	1,408	1,531	2,008	1,352
France	78	78	85	86	1,974	2,013	2,187	1,580
Germany	50	67	77	67	1,477	1,960	2,142	1,655
Greece	–	72	81	86	–	1,700	2,117	1,495
Ireland	57	63	74	82	2,211	2,418	2,482	1,819
Italy	67	71	72	80	2,103	2,164	2,324	1,678
Luxembourg	70	76	80	82	474	619	569	746
Netherlands	72	85	92	92	1,314	1,655	1,814	1,230
Portugal	–	55	47	60	–	838	2,141	1,630
Spain	–	65	69	78	–	604	2,132	1,720
UK	39	44	45	55	2,475	2,663	2,751	2,128
Mean EU 9 (unweighted)	64	71	77	81				
Mean EU 9 (weighted)	60	67	71	73				
CV	0.19	0.16	0.17	0.15				
CV (w)	0.25	0.19	0.21	0.17				
SD	12.2	11.1	12.9	12.2				
SD (w)	14.9	12.8	15.2	12.5				
max/min	2.0	1.9	2.1	1.7				

Notes: Eurobarometer surveys are carried out every six months. Responses given by 16-24 year olds to the question 'How old were you when you left full-time education?' were pooled for five-year periods to increase sample sizes. Averages and dispersion measures are calculated for the EU 9 included in the surveys from the beginning. Weighted calculations use population 15-24 from Table F6. 1975 population data are used to weight 1975-79 data; 1980 for 1980-84; 1985 for 1985-89 and 1990 for 1990-94.

Source: Eurobarometer surveys: EB cumulative file and EB39, EB40, EB41, EB42

C6: Results from the Third International Mathematics and Science Study (1994/95)

	Mean scores				Per cent reaching international median			
	Maths 7th grade	Maths 8th grade	Science 7th grade	Science 8th grade	Maths 7th grade	Maths 8th grade	Science 7th grade	Science 8th grade
Austria	509	539	519	558	63	61	65	64
Belgium (Flemmish)	558	565	529	550	86	73	73	64
Belgium (French)	507	526	442	471	64	58	30	29
Denmark	465	502	439	478	44	47	30	32
France	492	538	451	498	58	63	34	37
Germany	484	509	499	531	52	49	57	54
Greece	440	484	449	497	32	37	34	38
Ireland	500	527	495	538	60	57	54	57
Netherlands	516	541	517	560	69	63	67	67
Portugal	423	454	428	480	19	19	22	28
Spain	448	487	477	517	32	36	46	47
Sweden	477	519	488	535	50	53	51	56
England	476	506	512	552	47	48	60	60
Scotland	463	498	468	517	43	44	42	48

Notes: Finland and Luxembourg did not participate. Italy was 'unable to complete the steps necessary for their data to appear' in the TIMSS Report. See source for detailed notes on sampling procedure etc.

Source: Maths from Beaton et al (1996a, Tables 1.1 and 1.2: mean scores; Tables 1.4 and 1.5: share reaching international median). Science from Beaton et al (1996b, Tables 1.1 and 1.2: mean scores; Tables 1.4 and 1.5: share reaching international median)

D Teenage fertility

D1: Births to 15-19 year olds per 1,000 in the age group

	1960	1965	1970	1975	1980	1985	1990	1995
Austria	47.0	56.7	61.4	48.1	35.3	24.8	20.8	17.5
Belgium	34.7	41.7	43.2	39.0	28.2	17.6	11.4	9.2
Denmark	59.4	66.9	46.0	38.1	23.9	12.9	13.0	8.7
Finland	28.4	33.7	32.2	27.5	18.9	13.8	12.4	9.8
France	31.9	39.0	37.6	35.2	24.8	16.1	12.5	9.6
Germany	33.2	43.1	48.3	28.5	20.5	11.6	18.6	13.0
Greece	17.4	27.1	36.9	46.5	52.6	36.4	19.9	12.9
Ireland	8.8	14.0	16.3	22.8	23.0	16.6	16.5	15.1
Italy	19.1	25.3	27.1	32.5	20.6	12.1	8.6	7.0
Luxembourg	32.6	40.3	38.9	33.6	23.5	15.0	17.5	10.6
Netherlands	16.3	22.6	23.2	12.8	9.3	6.8	8.1	5.8
Portugal	26.6	25.8	29.8	37.0	41.0	32.4	24.3	20.2
Spain	9.6	11.1	13.8	21.4	25.6	18.3	11.9	8.3
Sweden	33.5	49.3	34.0	28.8	15.8	11.1	14.0	8.6
UK	33.8	45.1	49.7	36.7	30.6	29.6	32.4	28.5
Mean (unweighted)	28.8	36.1	35.9	32.6	26.2	18.3	16.1	12.3
Mean (weighted)	27.2	34.7	36.4	29.8	24.9	18.5	16.5	10.7
CV	0.45	0.41	0.35	0.28	0.39	0.45	0.39	0.47
CV (w)	0.37	0.37	0.34	0.23	0.30	0.43	0.48	0.55
SD	13.0	14.9	12.5	9.0	10.2	8.3	6.2	5.8
SD (w)	10.2	12.7	12.4	7.3	7.5	7.7	7.9	7.2
max/min	6.7	6.0	4.4	3.8	5.7	5.3	4.0	4.9

Notes: The 1960 data point for Austria actually refers to 1959; 1995 data for Italy and Spain are for 1994. Birth rates are calculated as live births per 1,000 women aged 15 to 19. Data for Austria, Finland and Sweden, and all data for 1990 and 1995 include births to women under 15. (Denominator is still female population 15-19.) For Greece, Spain, Ireland, Italy, Portugal, the UK, Austria, Sweden and Finland the definition of mother's age was age at last birthday. For Belgium, Denmark, Germany, France, Luxembourg and the Netherlands for 1960 to 1985, and for Germany and France also for 1990 and 1995, the definition given was mother's age reached during the calendar year in which the birth occurred. For these countries for these years, data were converted to be comparable with data using age at last birthday using the average ratio (for each country) of the two different birth rates over the period 1990-95 (both definitions were available for these years). As there were no German data on the age at last birthday, the conversion was made using the average of the ratio for all countries across the period 1990-95 (1.35). France 1990 and 1995 figures were obtained in the same way using the average ratio for France 1991-93 (1.39). Data for Germany for 1960-85 refer to the Federal Republic of Germany; data for 1990 and 1995 refer to the united Germany. 1960 to 1975 data for the UK refer to Great Britain only; ie Northern Ireland is excluded. Weighted calculations use female population 15-19 from Table F4.

Source: Data for 1960-85 with the exceptions of Austria, Finland and Sweden are from Eurostat (1990); data for Austria, Finland and Sweden are from UN (1979) (1960-75) and UN (1987) (1980 and 1985). Data for 1990 and 1995 were calculated from Eurostat (1997f)

D2: Births to 15-19 year olds as a share of total births (%)

	1960	1970	1980	1990	1995
Austria	9.9	13.6	12.3	5.9	4.4
Belgium	6.7	10.9	8.8	3.0	2.4
Denmark	14.7	11.8	8.0	3.7	2.0
Finland	6.3	10.3	5.6	2.8	2.5
France	6.4	9.4	6.6	3.5	2.4
Germany	6.3	11.6	8.4	4.6	3.5
Greece	3.5	8.4	12.6	7.2	4.7
Ireland	1.7	3.3	4.9	5.1	5.1
Italy	3.8	5.6	6.9	3.2	2.5
Luxembourg	6.4	10.6	8.1	3.9	2.1
Netherlands	3.1	5.3	3.2	2.2	1.4
Portugal	5.2	6.7	10.8	8.6	7.5
Spain	1.8	2.8	6.9	4.8	3.6
Sweden	9.5	8.1	4.5	3.1	2.1
UK	6.8	10.4	9.3	7.9	6.5
Mean (unweighted)	6.1	8.6	7.8	4.6	3.5
Mean (weighted)	5.5	8.4	7.7	4.7	3.7
CV	0.54	0.36	0.34	0.41	0.49
CV (w)	0.43	0.36	0.24	0.38	0.44
SD	3.3	3.1	2.6	1.9	1.7
SD (w)	2.3	3.0	1.9	1.8	1.6
max/min	8.9	4.9	4.0	3.9	5.4

Notes: Data for Austria, Finland and Sweden 1960 to 1980 are for births to women under 20 as a share of births to women of all ages. All data for 1990 and 1995 are for births to women under 20 as a share of births to women aged 15-49. Weighted calculations use female population aged 15-19 from Table F4.

Source: Calculated from teen birth rates in Table D1, and total birth rates and population figures given in matching sources; see Table D1 for further detail and notes

D3: Abortions per 1,000 females aged 15-19 (1990)

	1990
Austria	–
Belgium	–
Denmark	24.2
Finland	13.9
France	13.3
Germany	9.6
Greece	1.4
Ireland	–
Italy	5.8
Luxembourg	–
Netherlands	4.5
Portugal	–
Spain	3.1
Sweden	25.1
UK	21.8

Notes: Data presented are the total number of abortions to all females under 20 divided by the female population aged 15-19. For several EU countries no abortion data are published; in most cases this is because abortion remains illegal or very difficult to obtain legally. For example, in Belgium abortion is legal only in cases of 'state of distress/emergency'. In Ireland it is legal if the life of the woman is at risk, but no abortions are yet known to have been carried out and each woman would probably need court permission. In Portugal abortion is allowed in case of rape or serious threat to life, but most doctors are conscientious objectors and in practice the majority of abortions are still performed illegally. Conscientious objection is also an obstacle in Luxembourg, where abortion is in principle available up to 12 weeks but very difficult to obtain in practice; many women travel to the Netherlands to abort. In Austria abortion is available on request to 12 weeks but no data are published. (See 'Abortion Legislation in Europe' available from the International Planned Parenthood Federation, European Network; further details at www.ippf.org/regions/europe.)

Source: Calculated from data on number of abortions to 15-19 year olds in WHO *Health for all database* and population data in Table F4

D4: Share of teen births which are to unmarried mothers (1995) (%)

	1995
Austria	65
Belgium	45
Denmark	79
Finland	80
France	82
Germany	56
Greece	13
Ireland	94
Italy	37
Luxembourg	37
Netherlands	53
Portugal	46
Spain	46
Sweden	81
UK	86
Mean (unweighted)	60
Mean (weighted)	80

Notes: Data for Italy, France and Spain are for 1994; for Belgium 1992. Weighted calculations use female population aged 15-19 from Table F4.

Source: Calculated from Eurostat (1997f)

**D5: Birth rates to 16 year olds and to 19 year olds (1994)
(births per 1,000 in age group)**

	16 yrs	19 yrs	15-19 yrs
Austria	5.8	42.1	18.9
Belgium	2.5	23.3	9.3
Denmark	2.0	24.4	9.2
Finland	2.0	29.4	10.1
France	2.9	23.7	10.0
Germany	5.3	32.5	13.7
Greece	5.3	31.8	14.2
Ireland	5.3	33.0	14.6
Italy	3.1	15.4	7.0
Luxembourg	2.4	32.5	11.8
Netherlands	2.2	16.1	6.9
Portugal	9.6	38.4	20.9
Spain	3.7	16.2	8.3
Sweden	2.1	24.4	9.5
UK	13.1	53.8	28.8
Mean (unweighted)	4.5	29.1	12.9
Mean (weighted)	5.3	28.4	13.3
CV	0.68	0.35	0.45
CV (w)	0.68	0.45	0.54
SD	3.1	10.1	5.8
SD (w)	3.6	12.8	7.2
max/min	6.5	3.5	4.2

Notes: Birth rates are calculated as live births to women aged 16 (or 19) at last birthday, over female population aged 16 (or 19). French and German data are constructed from data for mother's age at end of calendar year as explained in notes to Table D1. Weighted calculations use female population aged 15-19 from Table F4. Note that data given here are for 1994; hence slight differences between 15-19 year old birth rates in this table and those in Table D1, where data were for 1995. (Data for 1995 were not available for all countries with breakdown of age by single years.)

Source: Calculated from the Eurostat (1997c)

E Life satisfaction

E1: Percentage of 15-19 year olds 'very' or 'fairly' satisfied with their lives

	1975 -79	1980 -84	1985 -89	1990 -94	Sample sizes 1975 -79	1980 -84	1985 -89	1990 -94
Belgium	94	92	89	89	833	640	834	748
Denmark	97	97	96	98	571	629	839	598
France	76	83	88	86	705	776	995	855
Germany	82	83	86	88	795	936	1,158	804
Greece	–	68	71	75	–	788	998	761
Ireland	87	84	83	90	1,214	1,087	1,491	1,243
Italy	62	74	82	87	1,047	991	1,238	1,138
Luxembourg	89	90	94	97	129	244	274	504
Netherlands	96	97	95	99	485	767	769	641
Portugal	–	–	80	87	–	–	1,123	1,065
Spain	–	–	84	85	–	–	1,188	1,118
UK	90	88	88	91	1,023	1,012	1,435	1,201
EU 9 (unweighted)	86	88	89	92				
EU 9 (weighted)	80	84	87	89				
CV	0.12	0.08	0.05	0.05				
CV (w)	0.14	0.07	0.04	0.04				
SD	10.6	6.9	4.8	4.7				
SD (w)	11.0	6.3	3.3	3.2				
max/min	1.6	1.3	1.2	1.2				

Notes: Eurobarometer surverys are six-monthly surveys of European public opinion and attitudes carried out since 1970. The life satisfaction question, 'On the whole, are you very/fairly/not very/not at all satisfied with the life you lead?' was asked regularly between 1974 and 1994. The data presented here pools responses for the five-year intervals shown in order to increase sample sizes. Only EU member states are included in the surveys, hence full time-series are available only for the EU 9. The Eurobarometer datasets include a EUROPEAN WEIGHT variable that adjusts each national sample in proportion to its country's share in the total population of all EU countries. This weight variable also incorporates within-country weighting information for Denmark, Spain, Germany, France, the Netherlands and the UK to make the samples from these countries nationally representative. The sample sizes given above show the full (unweighted) sample sizes for each country, but the percentages in each satisfaction category were calculated using the weights. For simplicity, weighted averages and dispersion measures were then calculated using the percentages given and the population figures in Table F3. Averages and dispersion measures are calculated only for the EU 9 for which four data points are available. Germany refers to the united Germany in 1993 and 1994; to the FRG previously. The question on satisfaction was asked in only one of the two surveys carried out in 1979, 1980 and 1981. It was not asked in Greece in 1980, nor in Spain and Portugal until 1985.

Source: Calculated from Eurobarometer surveys: EBCUM, EB39, EB40, EB41, EB42 (Inglehart et al, 1994; INRA, 1993a, 1993b, 1994a, 1994b)

E2: Percentage of 15-64 year olds 'very' or 'fairly' satisfied with their lives

	1975 -79	1980 -84	1985 -89	1990 -94	Sample sizes			
					1975 -79	1980 -84	1985 -89	1990 -94
Belgium	91	84	83	88	7,810	6,817	10,326	8,446
Denmark	95	96	95	97	7,292	6,664	9,869	8,481
France	71	73	74	75	8,802	6,951	10,140	8,539
Germany	84	84	86	88	7,368	7,228	10,747	12,116
Greece	–	63	66	55	–	6,133	10,024	8,449
Ireland	88	84	79	86	7,725	7,149	10,218	8,522
Italy	61	67	72	78	8,532	7,834	11,040	8,761
Luxembourg	89	92	93	95	2,286	2,184	3,156	3,904
Netherlands	93	93	93	94	7,623	7,234	10,363	8,700
Portugal	–	–	67	71	–	–	9,150	8,198
Spain	–	–	74	75	–	–	8,891	8,385
UK	85	86	86	86	10,208	9,113	12,948	11,087
EU 9 (unweighted)	84	84	85	87				
EU 9 (weighted)	78	79	81	83				
CV	0.13	0.11	0.09	0.08				
CV (w)	0.14	0.11	0.09	0.07				
SD	10.6	8.9	7.8	7.0				
SD (w)	10.9	8.7	7.2	6.1				
max/min	1.57	1.44	1.32	1.30				

Notes: As Table E1. Weighted calculations use total populations in Table F8.

Source: As Table E1

E3: Ratio of percentage of 15-19 year olds 'very' or 'fairly' satisfied to percentage of 15-64 year olds in this category

	1975-79	1980-84	1985-89	1990-94
Belgium	1.03	1.10	1.08	1.02
Denmark	1.03	1.02	1.01	1.01
France	1.07	1.14	1.18	1.14
Germany	0.98	0.99	1.00	1.00
Greece	–	1.09	1.08	1.36
Ireland	0.99	1.01	1.04	1.05
Italy	1.03	1.11	1.14	1.12
Luxembourg	1.00	0.98	1.02	1.03
Netherlands	1.04	1.04	1.01	1.05
Portugal	–	–	1.21	1.22
Spain	–	–	1.12	1.13
UK	1.05	1.03	1.02	1.05
EU 9 (unweighted)	1.02	1.05	1.06	1.05
EU 9 (weighted)	1.03	1.07	1.08	1.07
CV	0.03	0.05	0.06	0.04
CV (w)	0.03	0.05	0.07	0.05
SD	0.03	0.05	0.06	0.05
SD (w)	0.03	0.06	0.07	0.06
max/min	1.09	1.16	1.18	1.14

Source: Tables E1 and E2 above. Weighted calculations use total populations in Table F8

F Population

F1: Population aged under 5 (000s)

	1970	1975	1980	1985	1990	1995
Austria	608	498	430	453	444	473
Belgium	720	657	604	584	592	615
Denmark	388	362	314	276	287	335
Finland	348	302	320	325	309	328
France	4,205	4,118	3,699	3,788	3,783	3,626
Germany	4,715	3,381	2,931	2,986	4,373	4,191
Greece	770	690	718	688	550	519
Ireland	311	348	347	354	285	259
Italy	4,589	4,318	3,617	3,055	2,800	2,770
Luxembourg	24	23	21	21	23	27
Netherlands	1,188	1,027	885	873	927	989
Portugal	892	820	838	712	572	557
Spain	3,209	3,317	3,362	2,542	2,096	1,935
Sweden	581	551	487	427	540	606
UK	4,519	3,967	3,387	3,610	3,820	3,856
EU total	27,067	24,379	21,960	20,694	21,401	21,084

Note: Population as of January 1st of year in question. Data for Germany are for FRG until 1985 and for the united Germany for 1990 and 1995.

Source: 1970 to 1985 from UN (1991); 1990 and 1995 from Eurostat (1997f)

F2: Population aged 5-14 (000s)

	1960	1965	1970	1975	1980	1985	1990	1995
Austria	986	1,057	1,210	1,262	1,112	925	898	943
Belgium	1,404	1,481	1,558	1,524	1,381	1,251	1,209	1,212
Denmark	788	739	760	782	754	678	593	566
Finland	934	844	785	735	651	626	653	645
France	8,042	8,263	8,400	8,476	8,307	7,483	7,605	7,760
Germany	7,478	8,290	9,343	9,905	8,256	6,247	8,266	9,104
Greece	1,452	1,457	1,416	1,470	1,481	1,427	1,428	1,266
Ireland	579	582	610	644	694	702	675	628
Italy	8,241	8,034	8,636	9,118	8,953	8,126	6,721	5,851
Luxembourg	42	49	51	55	49	42	43	47
Netherlands	2,289	2,259	2,369	2,433	2,273	1,946	1,788	1,850
Portugal	1,678	1,686	1,709	1,719	1,696	1,677	1,495	1,226
Spain	5,337	5,690	6,229	6,512	6,614	6,400	5,760	4,674
Sweden	1,142	1,065	1,095	1,144	1,141	1,044	982	1,057
UK	8,039	7,884	8,972	9,154	8,383	7,286	7,053	7,505
EU total	48,431	49,380	53,143	54,933	51,745	45,860	45,170	44,333

Source and note as for Table F1

F3: Population aged 15-19 (000s)

	1970	1975	1980	1985	1990	1995
Austria	502	583	657	619	527	459
Belgium	725	779	796	717	670	613
Denmark	373	370	396	392	367	328
Finland	426	399	382	351	301	328
France	4,201	4,236	4,299	4,265	4,331	3,785
Germany	3,996	4,520	5,218	4,902	4,615	4,257
Greece	660	705	725	775	759	768
Ireland	258	292	321	330	328	338
Italy	3,857	4,058	4,569	4,741	4,377	3,696
Luxembourg	24	27	28	26	22	22
Netherlands	1,110	1,171	1,254	1,232	1,107	922
Portugal	780	797	905	860	836	807
Spain	2,655	2,947	3,182	3,284	3,314	3,185
Sweden	553	536	569	578	566	512
UK	3,893	4,159	4,596	4,540	4,005	3,442
EU total	24,013	25,579	27,897	27,612	26,127	23,461

Source and note as for Table F1

F4: Female population aged 15-19 (000s)

	1960	1965	1970	1975	1980	1985	1990	1995
Austria	273	245	247	287	325	303	258	222
Belgium	269	347	355	380	390	350	327	300
Denmark	186	202	181	180	193	190	179	160
Finland	175	237	208	195	187	172	147	160
France	1,361	2,029	2,062	2,080	2,112	2,085	2,117	1,852
Germany	1,987	1,786	1,952	2,198	2,531	2,384	2,248	2,068
Greece	311	355	323	343	351	373	369	373
Ireland	114	126	126	143	157	161	161	165
Italy	1,858	2,059	1,890	1,992	2,242	2,327	2,143	1,811
Luxembourg	10	11	12	14	14	13	11	11
Netherlands	446	577	542	573	613	602	542	451
Portugal	378	405	388	394	436	422	412	397
Spain	1,227	1,301	1,322	1,456	1,559	1,594	1,617	1,556
Sweden	291	306	270	261	278	282	277	250
UK	1,760	2,094	1,896	2,024	2,248	2,212	1,944	1,671
EU total	10,646	12,080	11,774	12,520	13,636	13,470	12,754	11,448

Source and note as for Table F1

F5: Population aged under 20 (000s)

	1970	1975	1980	1985	1990	1995
Austria	2,325	2,343	2,192	1,998	1,870	1,874
Belgium	3,005	2,960	2,780	2,551	2,471	2,440
Denmark	1,520	1,514	1,461	1,346	1,247	1,229
Finland	1,556	1,436	1,353	1,302	1,264	1,300
France	16,814	16,829	16,292	15,536	15,720	15,171
Germany	18,054	17,806	16,381	14,135	17,254	17,552
Greece	2,851	2,864	2,924	2,890	2,737	2,553
Ireland	1,184	1,284	1,359	1,386	1,287	1,225
Italy	17,080	17,493	17,125	15,922	13,898	12,317
Luxembourg	100	103	97	92	88	97
Netherlands	4,672	4,631	4,410	4,051	3,822	3,760
Portugal	3,368	3,336	3,429	3,248	2,903	2,590
Spain	12,108	12,777	13,148	12,225	11,170	9,794
Sweden	2,229	2,231	2,197	2,049	2,088	2,175
UK	17,359	17,280	16,363	15,436	14,878	14,802
EU total	104,225	104,887	101,511	94,167	92,698	88,878

Source and note as for Table F1

F6: Population aged 15-24 (000s)

	1970	1975	1980	1985	1990	1995
Austria	1,011	1,099	1,248	1,278	1,183	1,032
Belgium	1,443	1,528	1,587	1,509	1,411	1,299
Denmark	788	745	766	789	769	702
Finland	874	819	766	716	655	631
France	8,318	8,482	8,527	8,562	8,603	8,083
Germany	7,721	8,760	9,881	10,195	11,140	9,298
Greece	1,294	1,343	1,422	1,501	1,529	1,557
Ireland	470	536	590	620	595	626
Italy	7,952	7,876	8,611	9,359	8,997	8,139
Luxembourg	47	54	58	56	51	48
Netherlands	2,295	2,301	2,456	2,503	2,371	2,067
Portugal	1,501	1,533	1,725	1,714	1,608	1,635
Spain	5,179	5,601	6,061	6,547	6,551	6,496
Sweden	1,214	1,101	1,125	1,165	1,179	1,097
UK	8,177	8,050	8,721	9,287	8,640	7,502
EU total	48,284	49,828	53,544	55,801	55,281	50,214

Source and note as for Table F1

F7: Male population aged 15-24 (000s)

	1970	1975	1980	1985	1990	1995
Austria	515	556	629	649	604	526
Belgium	737	783	810	770	721	662
Denmark	405	382	392	404	394	358
Finland	448	419	392	372	334	322
France	4,252	4,315	4,327	4,340	4,369	4,108
Germany	3,949	4,461	5,097	5,243	5,713	4,778
Greece	665	694	728	780	777	799
Ireland	240	274	301	317	303	320
Italy	4,043	3,999	4,371	4,757	4,577	4,146
Luxembourg	24	27	29	28	26	25
Netherlands	1,177	1,175	1,254	1,278	1,210	1,052
Portugal	743	766	890	867	813	827
Spain	2,614	2,809	3,080	3,346	3,347	3,320
Sweden	621	563	575	596	604	560
UK	4,167	4,124	4,454	4,740	4,430	3,852
EU total	24,600	25,347	27,329	28,487	28,222	25,653

Source and note as for Table F1

F8. Total population (000s)

	1970	1975	1980	1985	1990	1995
Austria	7,467	7,579	7,549	7,558	7,690	8,040
Belgium	9,656	9,796	9,852	9,858	9,948	10,131
Denmark	4,929	5,060	5,123	5,122	5,135	5,216
Finland	4,606	4,711	4,780	4,902	4,974	5,099
France	50,772	52,699	53,880	55,170	56,577	58,020
Germany	60,651	61,829	61,566	61,024	79,113	81,539
Greece	8,793	9,047	9,643	9,934	10,121	10,443
Ireland	2,954	3,177	3,401	3,552	3,507	3,595
Italy	53,822	55,441	56,434	57,141	56,694	57,269
Luxembourg	339	362	364	367	379	407
Netherlands	13,032	13,653	14,144	14,484	14,893	15,424
Portugal	9,044	9,093	9,766	10,157	9,920	9,912
Spain	33,779	35,596	37,542	38,602	38,826	39,177
Sweden	8,043	8,193	8,310	8,350	8,527	8,816
UK	55,632	56,226	56,330	56,618	57,456	58,500
EU total	323,519	332,462	338,684	342,839	363,760	371,587

Source and note as for Table F1

References

Adamson, P. (1996) 'Beyond basics', in UNICEF, *The progress of nations, 1996*, New York, NY: UNICEF, pp 42-3.

Allen, I. (1991) *Family planning and pregnancy counselling projects for young people*, London: Policy Studies Institute.

Anand, S. and Ravallion, M. (1993) 'Human development in poor countries: on the role of private incomes and public services', *Journal of Economic Perspectives*, vol 7, no 1, pp 133-50.

Argyle, M. (1989) *The psychology of happiness*, London: Routledge.

Atkinson, A.B. (1995) 'Poverty, statistics and progress in Europe', in A.B. Atkinson, *Incomes and the welfare state: Essays on Britain and Europe*, Cambridge: Cambridge University Press, pp 64-77.

Atkinson, A.B. (1998a) *EMU, macroeconomics and children*, Innocenti Occasional Papers, No EPS 68, Florence: UNICEF International Child Development Centre.

Atkinson, A.B. (1998b) *Poverty in Europe*, Oxford: Basil Blackwell.

Atkinson, A.B. (1998c) 'Social exclusion, poverty and unemployment', in A.B. Atkinson and J. Hills (eds) *Exclusion, employment and opportunity*, CASE Paper No 4, London: Centre for Analysis of Social Exclusion, STICERD, London School of Economics.

Atkinson, A.B., Rainwater, L. and Smeeding, T. (1995) 'Income distribution in European countries', in A.B. Atkinson, *Incomes and the welfare state: Essays on Britain and Europe*, Cambridge: Cambridge University Press, pp 41-63.

Baumol, W.J. (1986) 'Productivity growth, convergence and welfare: what the long-run data show', *American Economic Review*, vol 76, no 5, pp 1072-85.

Beaton, A.E., Mullis, I.V.S., Martin, M.O., Gonzalez, E.J., Kelly, D.L. and Smith, T.A. (1996a) *Mathematics achievement in the middle school years: IEA's Third International Mathematics and Science Study*, Chestnut Hill, MA: Centre for the Study of Testing, Evaluation and Educational Policy, Boston College.

Beaton, A.E., Martin, M.O., Mullis, I.V.S., Gonzalez, E.J., Smith, T.A. and Kelly, D.L. (1996b) *Science achievement in the middle school years: IEA's Third International Mathematics and Science Study*, Chestnut Hill, MA: Centre for the Study of Testing, Evaluation and Educational Policy, Boston College.

Ben-Arieh, A. and Wintersberger, H. (eds) (1997) *Monitoring and measuring the state of children: Beyond survival*, Eurosocial Reports No 62, Vienna: European Centre.

Blanchflower, D.G. and Oswald, A.J. (1997) *The rising well-being of the young*, Discussion Paper Series on the Labour Market Consequences of Technical and Structural Change, No 16, Oxford: Centre for Economic Performance, London School of Economics, and Institute of Economics and Statistics, University of Oxford.

Bradbury, B. and Jäntti, M. (1999) *Child poverty across industrialized nations*, Innocenti Occasional Papers, Economic and Social Policy Series No 71, Florence: UNICEF International Child Development Centre.

Brown, B. (1998) 'Tracking the well-being of children within states: the evolving Federal role in the age of devolution', *New Federalism: Issues and Options for States*, No A-21 http://www.urban.org, The Urban Institute.

Bury, J. (1984) *Teenage pregnancy in Britain*, London: Birth Control Trust.

Butler, M., Ineichen, B., Taylor, B. and Wadsworth, J. (1981) *Teenage mothering: Report to the Department of Health and Social Security*, Bristol: University of Bristol.

Callan, T. and Nolan, B. (1997) *Income distribution and socioeconomic differences in international perspective*, Dublin: The Economic and Social Research Institute.

Charlton, J., Kelly, S., Dunnell, K., Evans, B., Jenkins, R. and Wallis, R. (1992) 'Trends in suicide deaths in England and Wales', *Population Trends*, No 69 (Autumn), pp 10-16.

Clark, A.E. and Oswald, A.J. (1994) 'Unhappiness and unemployment', *Economic Journal*, vol 104, no 424, pp 648-59.

Commission on Social Justice/IPPR (Institute for Public Policy Research) (1994) *Social justice, strategies for national renewal: The Report of the Commission on Social Justice*, London: Vintage.

Cossey, D. (1997) 'Women's choices: abortion and the New Europe', *Choices: Sexual Health and Family Planning in Europe*, vol 26, no 2.

Council of Europe (1996) 'Recommendation 1286 (1996) on a European Strategy for Children', EREC1286WP, 1403-24/1/96-16-E, Strasbourg: Council of Europe Parliamentary Assembly.

CSO (Central Statistical Office) (1994) *Social focus on children*, London: HMSO.

DeLong, J.B. (1988) 'Productivity growth, convergence and welfare: comment', *American Economic Review*, vol 78, no 5, pp 1138-54.

DHHS (Department of Health and Human Services) (1996) *Trends in the well-being of America's children and youth*, Washington, DC: DHHS.

Diekstra, R.F.W., Kienhorst, C.W.M. and de Wilde, E.J. (1995) 'Suicide and suicidal behaviour among adolescents', in M. Rutter and D.J. Smith (eds) *Psychosocial disorders in young people: Time trends and their causes*, Chichester: Academia Europaea and John Wiley and Sons, pp 686-761.

Ditch, J., Barnes, H., Bradshaw, J. and Kilkey, M. (eds) (1998) *Developments in national family policies in 1996*, Brussels: The European Observatory on National Family Policies, Commission of the European Communities.

DoH (Department of Health) (1992) *The health of a nation: A strategy for health in England*, London: HMSO.

Dowrick, S. and Nguyen, D.T. (1989) 'OECD comparative economic growth, 1950-85: catch-up and convergence', *American Economic Review*, vol 79, no 5, pp 1010-30.

Durkheim, E. ([1897] 1956) *Suicide: A study in sociology*, London: Routledge and Kegan Paul.

Easterlin, R.A. (1974) 'Does economic growth improve the human lot? Some empirical evidence', in P.A. David and M.W. Reder (eds) *Nations and households in economic growth*, New York, NY: Academic Press.

European Commission (1996) *First report on economic and social cohesion, 1996*, Luxembourg: Office for Official Publications of the European Communities.

Eurostat (1990) *Demographic Statistics 1990*, Luxembourg: Office for Official Publications of the European Communities.

Eurostat (1996) *A social portrait of Europe,* Luxembourg: Office for Official Publications of the European Communities.

Eurostat (1997a) *Youth in the European Union: From education to working life,* Luxembourg: Office for Official Publications of the European Communities.

Eurostat (1997b) *Key data on education in the European Union,* Luxembourg: Office for Official Publications of the European Communities.

Eurostat (1997c) *Demographic Statistics 1997,* Luxembourg: Office for Official Publications of the European Communities.

Eurostat (1997d) *Eurostat Yearbook '97: A statistical eye on Europe 1986-1996,* Luxembourg: Office for Official Publications of the European Communities.

Eurostat (1997e) *Statistics in focus: Population and social conditions,* No 6, Luxembourg: Office for Official Publications of the European Communities.

Eurostat (1997f) *Demographic Statistics 1997: Diskette version with Cub.X Software,* Luxembourg: Office for Official Publications of the European Communities.

Eurostat (1997g) *Education across the EU: Statistics and indicators,* Luembourg: Office for Official Publications of the European Communities.

Eurostat (1998a) *Statistics in Focus: Population and social conditions,* No 15, Luxembourg: Office for Official Publications of the European Communities.

Eurostat (1998b) *Statistics in Focus: Population and social conditions,* No 11, Luxembourg: Office for Official Publications of the European Communities.

Eurostat (1998c) *Labour Force Survey: Results 1997,* Luxembourg: Office for Official Publications of the European Communities.

Eurostat (1999) *Statistics in Focus: Population and social conditions,* No 3, Luxembourg: Office for Official Publications of the European Communities.

Federal Interagency Forum on Child and Family Statistics (1998) *America's children: Key national indicators of well-being, 1998,* Washington, DC: US Government Printing Office.

Forum for Family Planning (1994) *Can we learn from the Dutch? A report of a conference held in January 1994,* Cambridge: Organon Laboratories.

Furstenburg, F., Brooks-Gunn, J. and Morgan, S.P. (1987) *Adolescent mothers in later life,* Cambridge: Cambridge University Press.

Geronimus, A.T. (1987) 'On teenage childbearing and neonatal mortality in the United States', *Population and Development Review,* vol 13, no 2, pp 245-79.

Geronimus, A.T. and Korenman, S. (1992) 'The socioeconomic consequences of teen childbearing reconsidered', *Quarterly Journal of Economics,* vol 107, no 4, pp 1187-214.

Gregg, P. and Wadsworth, J. (1996) *It takes two: Employment polarization in the OECD,* Discussion Papers No 304, London: Centre for Economic Performance, London School of Economics.

Hagenaars, A., de Vos, K. and Zaidi, M.A. (1994) *Poverty statistics in the late 1980s: Research based on microdata,* Luxembourg: Office for Official Publications of the European Communities.

Hassall, I. (1997) 'Why are so many young people killing themselves?', *Butterworth's Family Law Journal* (New Zealand), September.

Hauser, R.M., Brown, B.V. and Prosser, W.R. (eds) (1997) *Indicators of children's well-being,* New York, NY: Russell Sage Foundation.

Hillman, M. (ed) (1993) *Children, transport and the quality of life,* London: Policy Studies Institute.

Hillman, M., Adams, J. and Whitelegg, J. (1990) *One false move: A study of children's independent mobility,* London: Policy Studies Institute.

Hofferth, S.L. and Moore, K.A. (1979) 'Early childbearing and later economic well-being', *American Sociological Review,* vol 44, pp 784-815.

Hoffman, Saul D., Foster, E.M. and Furstenberg, Jr, F.F. (1993) 'Reevaluating the costs of teenage childbearing', *Demography,* vol 30, no 1.

Hotz, V.J., Mullin, C.H. and Sanders, S.G. (1997) 'Bounding causal effects using data from a contaminated natural experiment: analysing the effects of teenage childbearing', *Review of Economic Studies,* vol 64, pp 575-603.

Huang, W.-C. (1996) 'Religion, culture, economic and sociological correlates of suicide rates: a cross-national analysis', *Applied Economics Letters*, vol 3, pp 779-82.

Inglehart, R., Reif, K. and Melich, A. (1994) *European Communities Studies, 1970-92: Cumulative file* (Computer file), 3rd ICPSR version, Ann Arbor, MI: Ronald Inglehart, University of Michigan [producer], 1994; Ann Arbor, MI: Inter-university Consortium for Political and Social Research [distributor], 1994; Cologne, Germany: Zentralarchiv für Empirische Sozialforschung [distributor], 1995.

INRA (International Research Associates) (1993a) *Eurobarometer 39.0* (Computer file), INRA, Brussels: Commission of the European Communities.

INRA (1993b) *Eurobarometer 40.0* (Computer file), INRA, Brussels: Commission of the European Communities.

INRA (1994a) *Eurobarometer 41.0* (Computer file), INRA, Brussels: Commission of the European Communities.

INRA (1994b) *Eurobarometer 42.0* (Computer file), INRA, Brussels: Commission of the European Communities.

Jacobson, L.D., Wilkinson, C. and Pill, R. (1995) 'Teenage pregnancy in the United Kingdom in the 1990s: the implications for primary care', *Family Practice*, vol 12, no 2, pp 232-6.

Jenkins, S.P. (1999) *Modelling household income dynamics*, Colchester: University of Essex: ESRC Research Centre on Micro-Social Change Working Paper 99-1.

Jones, E.F., Darroch Forrest, J., Henshaw, S.K., Silverman, J. and Torres, A. (1989) *Pregnancy, contraception and family planning services in industrialized countries: A study of the Alan Guttmacher Institute*, New Haven, CT: Yale University Press.

Jones, E.F., Darroch Forrest, J., Goldman, N., Henshaw, S., Lincoln, R., Rosoff, J.I., Westoff, C.F. and Wulf, D. (1986) *Teenage pregnancy in industrialized countries: A study sponsored by the Alan Guttmacher Institute*, New Haven, CT: Yale University Press.

Kiernan, K. (1995) *Transition to parenthood, young mothers, young fathers: Associated factors and later life experiences*, Welfare State Programme Discussion Papers No 113 London: STICERD, London School of Economics.

Kiernan, K. (1997) 'Becoming a young parent: a longitudinal study of associated factors', *British Journal of Sociology*, vol 48, no 3, pp 406-28.

Lester, D. (1992) *Why people kill themselves: A 1990s summary of research findings on suicidal behaviour*, 3rd edn, Springfield, IL: Charles C. Thomas.

Macintyre, S. and Cunningham-Burley, S. (1993) 'Teenage pregnancy as a social problem: a perspective from the UK', in A. Lawson and D.L. Rhode (eds) *The politics of pregnancy: Adolescent sexuality and public policy*, New Haven, CT: Yale University Press, pp 59-73.

Madge, N. (1999) 'Youth suicide in an international context', *European Child and Adolescent Psychiatry*, vol 8, no 4, pp 276-82.

Madge, N. and Harvey, J.G. (1999) 'Suicide among the young: the size of the problem', *Journal of Adolescence*, vol 22, no 1, pp 145-55.

Manlove, J. (1997) 'Early motherhood in an intergenerational perspective: the experiences of a British cohort', *Journal of Marriage and the Family*, vol 59, pp 263-79.

Maynard, R. (ed) (1997) *Kids having kids: Economic costs and social consequences of teen pregnancy*, Aldershot: Ashgate/Urban Institute Press.

Morrell, S.L., Taylor, R.J. and Kerr, C.B. (1998) 'Unemployment and young people's health', *Medical Journal of Australia*, vol 168, 2 March.

Murray, S. (1996) 'USA schools: money counts', *New Economy*, vol 3, no 4, pp 194-8.

OECD (Organisation for Economic Co-operation and Development) (1995) *Literacy, economy and society: Results of the First International Adult Literacy Survey*, Paris: OECD and Statistics Canada.

OECD (1996) *Employment outlook*, Paris: OECD.

OECD (1997a) *Literacy skills for the knowledge society: Further results from the International Adult Literacy Survey*, Paris: OECD, Human Resources Development Canada and Statistics Canada.

OECD (1997b) *Education at a glance: OECD indicators 1997*, Paris: OECD.

OECD (1998) *Employment outlook*, Paris: OECD.

Ohberg, A., Lonnqvist, J., Sarna, S. and Vuori, E. (1996) 'Violent methods associated with high suicide mortality among the young', *Journal of the American Academy of Child and Adolescent Psychiatry*, vol 35, no 2, pp 144-53.

Osbourne, G.K., Howat, R.C.L. and Jordan, M.M. (1981) 'The obstetric outcome of teenage pregnancy', *British Journal of Obstetrics and Gynaecology*, vol 88, pp 215-21.

Pescosolido, B.A. and Mendelsohn, R. (1986) 'Social causation or social construction of suicide? An investigation into the social organization of official rates', *American Sociological Review*, vol 51, pp 80-101.

Phoenix, A. (1991) *Young mothers*, Oxford: Polity Press.

Pissarides, C. (1981) 'Staying on at school in England and Wales', *Economica*, vol 48, pp 345-63.

Prais, S.J. (1997) 'How did English schools and pupils *really* perform in the 1995 International Comparisons in Mathematics?', *National Institute Economic Review*, no 161, pp 53-68.

Puryear, J.M. (1995) 'International education statistics and research: status and problems', *International Journal of Educational Development*, vol 15, no 1, pp 79-91.

Quah, D. (1997a) *Regional cohesion from Local Isolated Actions: I. Historical outcomes*, Discussion Papers No 378, London: Centre for Economic Performance, London School of Economics.

Quah, D. (1997b) *Regional cohesion from Local Isolated Actions: II. Conditioning*, Discussion Papers No 379, London: Centre for Economic Performance, London School of Economics.

Raiser, M. (1998) 'Subsidizing inequality: economic reforms, fiscal transfers and convergence across Chinese provinces', *Journal of Development Studies*, vol 34, no 3, pp 1-26.

Ribar, D.C. (1994) 'Teenage fertility and high school completion', *Review of Economics and Statistics*, vol 76, pp 413-24.

Rodman, H. and Trost, J. (eds) (1986) *The adolescent dilemma: International perspectives on the family planning rights of minors*, New York, NY: Praeger.

Rutter, M. and Smith, D.J. (eds) (1995) *Psychosocial disorders in young people: Time trends and their causes*, Chichester: Academia Europaea and John Wiley and Sons.

Ruxton, S. (1996) *Children in Europe*, London: NCH Action for Children.

Sala-i-Martin, X. (1996a) 'Regional cohesion: evidence and theories of regional growth and convergence', *European Economic Review*, vol 40, no 6, pp 1325-52.

Sala-i-Martin, X. (1996b) 'The classical approach to convergence analysis', *Economic Journal*, vol 106, no 437, pp 1019-36.

Saraceno, C. (1997) 'Growth, regional imbalance and child well-being: Italy over the last four decades', in G.A. Cornia and S. Danziger (eds) *Child poverty and deprivation in the industrialized countries, 1945-1995*, Oxford: Clarendon Press, pp 260-83.

Schofield, G. (1994) *The youngest mothers: The experience of pregnancy and motherhood among young women of school age*, Aldershot: Avebury.

Sen, A. (1985) *The standard of living*, The Tanner Lectures, Clare Hall, Cambridge: Cambridge University Press.

Sen, A. (1992) *Inequality reexamined*, Oxford: Clarendon Press.

Sen, A. (1998) 'Mortality as an indicator of economic success and failure', *Economic Journal*, vol 108, no 446, pp 1-25.

Sharpe, S. (1987) *Falling for love: Teenage mothers talk*, Virago Upstarts, UK: Little, Brown and Company.

Silva, M. (1997) 'Child welfare in Portugal amid fast growth and weak social policy', in G.A. Cornia and S. Danziger (eds) *Child poverty and deprivation in the industrialized countries, 1945-1995*, Oxford: Clarendon Press, pp 233-59.

Smith, T. (1993) 'Influence of socioeconomic factors on attaining targets for reducing teenage pregnancies', *British Medical Journal*, vol 306, pp 1,232-35.

Social Exclusion Unit (1999) *Teenage pregnancy*, Cm 4342, London: The Stationery Office.

South, S.J. (1984) 'Racial differences in suicide: the effect of economic convergence', *Social Science Quarterly*, vol 65, pp 172-80.

Streeten, P. and Burki, S. (1978) 'Basic needs: some issues', *World Development*, No 6.

Sykes, R. and Alcock, P. (1998) *Developments in European social policy: Convergence and diversity?*, Bristol: The Policy Press.

Taylor, S. (1982) *Durkheim and the study of suicide*, London: Macmillan.

The Samaritans (1996) *Suicide in the UK*, http://www.samaritans.org.uk: The Samaritans.

Toynbee, P. (1998) 'Why kids have babies', *The Guardian*, 26 August.

UN (United Nations) (1972) *Demographic Yearbook 1971*, New York, NY: UN.

UN (1973) *Demographic Yearbook 1972*, New York, NY: UN.

UN (1974) *Demographic Yearbook 1973*, New York, NY: UN.

UN (1979) *Demographic Yearbook: Historical supplement*, New York, NY: UN.

UN (1981) *Demographic Yearbook 1980*, New York, NY: UN.

UN (1986) *Demographic Yearbook 1985*, New York, NY: UN.

UN (1987) *Demographic Yearbook 1986*, New York, NY: UN.

UN (1991) *The sex and age distribution of the world populations: The 1990 revision*, New York, NY: UN.

UN (1994) *Demographic Yearbook 1992*, New York, NY: UN.

UN (1998) *Demographic Yearbook 1996*, New York, NY: UN.

UNDP (United Nations Development Programme) (1998) *Human Development Report, 1998*, New York, NY: Oxford University Press.

UNESCO (United Nations Educational, Scientific and Cultural Organisation) (1997) *Statistical Yearbook 1997*, Paris: UNESCO.

UNESCO (1998a) *Trends in compulsory education*, http://unescostat.unesco.org/Indicator/Indframe.htm, UNESCO.

UNESCO (1998b) *Age-specific enrolment ratios*, http://unescostat.unesco.org/Indicator/Indframe.htm, UNESCO.

UNICEF (1998) *The state of the world's children 1998*, New York, NY: Oxford University Press.

Valkonen, T. (1985) 'The mystery of the premature mortality of Finnish men', in R. Alapuro, M. Alestalo, E. Haavio-Mannila and R. Vayrynen (eds) *Small states in comparative perspective: Essays for Erik Allardt*, Oslo: Norwegian University Press, pp 228-41.

Viren, M. (1996) 'Suicide and business cycles: Finnish evidence', *Applied Economics Letters*, vol 3, pp 737-8.

Whitfield, K. and Wilson, R. (1991) 'Staying on in full-time education: the educational participation rate of 16-year-olds', *Economica*, vol 58, pp 391-404.

WHO (World Health Organisation) (1966) *World Health Statistics Annual 1965*, Geneva: WHO.

WHO (1967) *World Health Statistics Annual 1966*, Geneva: WHO.

WHO (1968) *World Health Statistics Annual 1967*, Geneva: WHO.

WHO (1972) *World Health Statistics Annual 1971*, Geneva: WHO.

WHO (1973) *World Health Statistics Annual 1972*, Geneva: WHO.

WHO (1974) *World Health Statistics Annual 1973*, Geneva: WHO.

WHO (1977) *World Health Statistics Annual 1976*, Geneva: WHO.

WHO (1978) *World Health Statistics Annual 1977*, Geneva: WHO.

WHO (1979) *World Health Statistics Annual 1978*, Geneva: WHO.

WHO (1982) *World Health Statistics Annual 1981*, Geneva: WHO.

WHO (1983) *World Health Statistics Annual 1982*, Geneva: WHO.

WHO (1984) *World Health Statistics Annual 1983*, Geneva: WHO.

WHO (1987) *World Health Statistics Annual 1986*, Geneva: WHO.

WHO (1988) *World Health Statistics Annual 1987*, Geneva: WHO.

WHO (1989) *World Health Statistics Annual 1988*, Geneva: WHO.

WHO (1992) *World Health Statistics Annual 1991*, Geneva: WHO.

WHO (1993) *World Health Statistics Annual 1992*, Geneva: WHO.

WHO (1994) *World Health Statistics Annual 1993*, Geneva: WHO.

WHO (1995) *World Health Statistics Annual 1994*, Geneva: WHO.

WHO (1996a) *World Health Statistics Annual 1995*, Geneva: WHO.

WHO (1996b) *The health of youth: A cross-national survey*, Geneva: WHO Regional Publications, European Series, No 69, Copenhagen: WHO Regional Office for Europe.

WHO (1998) *Health for all statistical database*, http://www.who.dk/country/country.htm, WHO Regional Office for Europe.

Wolkind, S.N. and Kruk, S. (1985) 'Teenage pregnancy and motherhood', *Journal of the Royal Society of Medicine*, vol 78, pp 112-16.

Wottiez, I. and Theeuwes, J. (1998) 'Well-being and labor market status', in S.P. Jenkins, A. Kapteyn and B.M.S. van Praag (eds) *The distribution of welfare and household production: International perspectives*, Cambridge: Cambridge University Press, pp 211-30.

Index

NOTE: Page numbers followed by *n* indicate information is to be found in a note; page numbers followed by *f* or *t* indicate information is to be found in a figure or a table respectively.